D0674474

THE
CITY of LONDON
COOKBOOK

PETER GLADWIN

Published by Accent Press Ltd – 2006
www.accentpress.co.uk

Recipes and articles © Individual contributors – 2006
Compilation © Accent Press – 2006

All rights reserved. No part of this book may be reproduced, stored in a retrieval system or transmitted in any form or by any means, electronic, electrostatic, magnetic tape, mechanical, photocopying, recording or otherwise, without the prior written permission of the publishers: Accent Press Ltd, PO Box 50, Pembroke Dock, Pembrokeshire SA72 6WY.

Printed and bound in the UK by Creative Print and Design Group, Harmondsworth, Middlesex.
Typeset by Ampersand

To Bridget

in appreciation of 25 years of both marriage
and putting up with my culinary adventures

LIST OF CONTRIBUTORS

John Allen . . . . .The Cutlers' Company
Herbert Berger . . . . .Chef
Tony Blair . . . . .The Prime Minister
Charles Boyd . . . . .Chef
Alex Buchanan . . . . .The Clothworkers' Company
David Cameron .Leader of the Opposition
Sir Menzies Campbell . . . . .Leader of The Liberal Democrats
Terence Conran . . . . .Designer and Restaurateur
B.J.N. Coombes . . . . .Guild of Parish Clerks
Josceline Dimbleby . . . . .Cookery Writer
Brett Dolman . . . . .Historic Royal Palaces
Dan Einzig . . . . .Mystery Design
Sir Robert and Lady Finch . . . . .Former Lord Mayor
Michel Giguel . . . . .Chef
Sir Alexander Graham . . . . .Former Lord Mayor
Charles Henty . . . . .The Old Bailey
HRH The Duke of Kent . . . . .The Royal Family
Lord Kingsdown . . . . . .Former Governor of The Bank of England
Ken Livingstone . . . . .The Mayor of London
Canon David Meara .Rector of St Bride's
Sir John Major . . . . .Former Prime Minister
Anton Mossimann . . . . .Chef
Brian Plummer . . . . .The Skinners' Company
Gordon Ramsay . . . . .Chef
The Remembrancers Department .Guildhall
Susie Robinson . . . . .Chef
Brigadier Smythe . . . . .The Vintners' Company
Rick Stein . . . . .Chef
Bernard Sullivan . . . . .Toastmaster
Roy Sully . . . . .The Butchers' Company
Giles Thompson . . . . .Chef
Jonathan Warner . . . . .Chef
Michael Winner . . . . .Film Producer and Critic
Antony Worrall Thompson . . . . .Chef

ACKNOWLEDGMENTS

The Lord Mayor and Lady Mayoress, David and Tessa Brewer, have been hugely supportive of this project from the very start and I have really appreciated their enthusiasm, encouragement and friendship.

My very grateful thanks must also go to all the lovely ladies who helped make this book possible. Vicky O'Hare who started the ball rolling; Hazel Cushion my ever enthusiastic publisher; Emma Spofforth who, thanks to her broken ankle, gave a month to researching, editing and collating the recipes; Sian Davies who did all the research, correspondence and mastered my appalling handwriting, and finally Olivia Stewart-Cox – still the most naturally talented chef I have ever known.

PETER GLADWIN

Peter Gladwin is a well known figure in the City of London where he has brought his unique style of modern British cooking to many historic occasions. From parading the Swan at "The Swan Feast" to carving the Baron of Beef at the Lord Mayor's Banquet, he has become a leading authority on City hospitality.

Peter has written two previous successful recipe books – The Entertaining Cook and Party Ingredients, both divulging his secrets for easy entertaining at home. He also presents cookery master-classes in aid of various charities and has regularly appeared on television and radio.

A prolific, totally hands-on chef, he enjoys the variety and challenge of different outlets, runs a group of restaurants and creates all of his own. Peter lives in West Sussex with his wife Bridget and three sons. They also own Nutbourne Vineyards producing a range of award winning English wines.

THE CITY OF LONDON COOKBOOK

CONTENTS

4. TUPPENCE A BAG
   - Watercress and Almond Soup
   - Terence Conran's Classic Fish Soup
   - Roasted Butternut Soup
   - Pheasant Poachers Soup with Pearl Barley
   - Gordon Ramsay's London Particular

5. ROAST SWAN AND FINE CLARET
   - Duck Confit and Cranberry Parcels with Spiced Broccoli Puree
   - Pan Roasted Quail with Puy Lentils, Lardon and Fresh Beetroot
   - Michaelmas Goose Salad with Cox's Apples and Cobb Nuts
   - Mixed Game and Juniper Terrine
   - Wood Pigeon Breasts with Black Pudding and Damson

6. DOING THE DEAL
   - Ballotine of Foie Gras with Honeycomb and Chargrilled Grapes
   - Dill Blini with Smoked Salmon, Créme Fraîche and Keta
   - Dressed Oysters with Ginger, Lime and Crispy Shallots
   - Prism's Langoustine and Baby Leek Terrine
   - Michael Winner's Scrambled Egg with Caviar

7. A CHINESE BANQUET!
   - Dover Sole with Red Chilli, Coriander and Steamed Bok Choy
   - Tiger Prawn and Mango Salad with Oriental Dressing
   - Sizzle Cooked Lamb in Lettuce Wraps
   - Seared Tuna with Cranberry Infusion
   - Thai Fish Cakes with Coconut Relish

8. FISH ON MONDAYS
   - Rick Stein's Crab Florentine
   - Anton Mossiman's Marinated Salmon and Crab with Lemon Dressing
   - Fillet of Sole with Minted Pea Puree and Balsamic
   - Medallions of Monkfish with Asparagus, Croutons and Mustard Seed Dressing
   - The Mansion House Devon Scallops with White Bean Broth

9. CRIME AND PUNISHMENT
   - Cod and Rocket Fish Cakes with Seasoned Créme Fraîche
   - Twice Baked Celeriac and Salmon Soufflé
   - Clam Chowder
   - Sir Menzies' Smoked Haddock Pie
   - Fillet of Seabass with Lemon Risotto

10. GOOD ENOUGH FOR ROYALTY
   - Tournedos of Beef Crowned with a Golden Artichoke Soufflé – Sage Butter Sauce
   - The Duke of Kent's Beef Stew
   - Breast of Duck with Raspberries, Red Onion and Tarragon
   - Lobster Thermidor
   - Anthony Worrall Thompson's Crown Roast of Lamb

11. CITY SKIES
   - Anton Mossiman's Poached Chicken filled with Baby Leeks and Trompette Mushrooms
   - Breast of Pheasant with Pancetta and Chestnut
   - Cannon of Lamb Steamed in Spinach
   - A Partridge in a Pear Tree
   - Calves Liver, Smoked Bacon and Onion Gravy

12. THE BARON OF BEEF

- Beef Wellington
- Milk Roasted Loin of Pork with Mustard and Honey
- Shank of Lamb with Red Onion, Apricot and Pinenuts
- Roast Beef, Yorkshire Pudding and Gravy
- Corn-fed Chicken infused with Orange and Rosemary

13. A WILD BOAR IN THE HEART OF THE CITY

- Charles Boyd's Oxtail Stew
- Wild Boar Chops with Caramelised Apples and Roquefort
- Terrence Conran's Steak and Kidney Pudding
- No.1 Lombard Street's Coq Au Vin
- Rack of Venison with Red Onion Marmalade

14. GOING TO MARKET

- Anton's Medley of Baby Market Vegetables
- Horseradish and Toasted Walnut Mash
- Antony Worrall Thompson's Ginger Carrots
- AWT's Fresh Peas, Spring Onion and Artichoke
- Asparagus and Bean Bundles
- Honey Roasted Parsnips, Turnips and Carrots
- Ken Livingstone's Roasted New Potatoes with Thyme
- Parsnip and Other Crisps
- Colcannon
- Celeriac and Apple Puree

15. BRIDGES FOR SALE – SAUCES REVEALED

- Hollandaise, Dijonnaise, Bernaise and Choron
- Balsamic Reduction
- Cumberland Sauce
- Scandinavian Mustard and Dill Sauce
- Tarragon Beurre Blanc
- Salsa Roja and Salsa Verdi
- Cream of Horseradish
- Tartare Sauce

FOREWORD

By
The Right Honourable The Lord Mayor of London
Alderman David Brewer CMG

As Lord Mayor of London for 2005/2006 I am delighted to be writing this foreword for The City of London Cookbook.

I am very grateful to Peter Gladwin and to all of the contributors for making this special book possible. There are some wonderful favourite recipes inside which I know will provide excellent inspiration in many a kitchen!

Peter and his company Party Ingredients Private Caterers have been an essential part of the City social scene for the last thirty years – from corporate receptions and formal Livery Company dinners, right through to expertly run State Banquets at Guildhall. I was delighted that they were the caterers who prepared the delicious dinner at my Lord Mayor's Banquet on 14th November 2005 and I am very pleased that Peter has now written this unique cookbook to raise money for my charity appeal as Lord Mayor.

My Appeal is all about giving opportunities to disabled children. Imagine being desperate to dance and not being able to move your legs. Imagine being eager to learn but not able to use your computer. Imagine having a head full of ideas and no voice. The Treloar Trust runs a school and a college which educate, enable and empower some of the most disabled young people in Britain today. My wife Tessa and I have been supporters for many years – as parents we appreciated on our first visit that the school and college are doing an amazing job at enabling physically disabled young people to develop independence, of spirit and of action, so that they can take control of their lives.

The Trust was founded by a former Lord Mayor – Lord Mayor Treloar, in 1906. Like me, he was a Cornishman. It took three years to get the original project up and running. For that reason, Treloar's Centenary Appeal will also last for three years with an ambitious target to raise £12 million to help the Trust prepare for its next hundred years. The money raised will go towards three important projects: providing a new Sixth Form Hall of Residence to fit the needs of electric wheelchair users and those who need increasingly complex equipment; new classrooms to accommodate bulky wheelchairs; and outreach workers to work with disabled young people once they graduate from the college. I call them 'Trelinks' – mentors who will enable students to make the transition from school and college to a productive and fulfilling adult life.

It is a wonderful cause and I thank everyone for supporting it.

With very best wishes Alderman David Brewer CMG
The Rt. Hon The Lord Mayor of London

INTRODUCTION

"I drink to you in a loving cup and bid you all a hearty welcome"
– the first toast welcoming guests to a formal City dinner.

My father's generation would refer to a businessman's profession as 'Something in the City' – a catch-all description of a cigar smoking, bowler-hatted gent who makes oodles of money with little effort in the City of London. That may not be the City of today but for centuries merchants, brokers, noblemen and commoners have done business in this compact "square mile" of Britain which has shaped the commercial world.

But is this city really all about finance and big business? Within the private domains of great banks, behind the iron gates of ancient Livery Halls and beyond the stylish entrances of fashionable restaurants, there lie kitchens and dining rooms galore: the real engine rooms of the metropolis. After all, was it not a Pudding Lane baker who in 1666 (presumably in a fit of peak) burnt down the entire City, thus bringing an end to the black plague? Stock deals worth millions are brokered over Foie Gras and vintage wine, not across stark boardroom tables. And who throws a soiree for The Royal Family every time they have something to celebrate? There are many faces to food and dining in the City of London and in this book I will try to give you a little insight into some of them.

All my working life I too have been 'Something in the City': a caterer for private events and parties, a Restaurateur and a chef for great banquets; it is surprising what you can find out looking through that crack in the green base kitchen door. My cook's-eye view covers snippets of history, odd facts and personal anecdotes, that I hope you will find both enlightening and entertaining. Within each chapter is a selection of City recipes. Some are wholly practical, which I hope will extend your culinary repertoire, whilst others, such as Michael Winner's Scrambled Egg with Beluga

Caviar or Sir John Major's Frozen Champagne are simply frivolous and fun.

The Lord Mayor and I have been delighted with the wonderful range of contributors who have provided recipes or information for this book and very grateful also to you for supporting the Treloar Trust by buying it. There is something very British about the way people in this country get behind good causes and we could not get over such busy people as The Prime Minister and Gordon Ramsay (which of them runs the country?) making the time to support this project.

The City of London is a truly fascinating place, full of history and tradition yet vibrant with the commerce of today. Whether you believe 'it marches on its stomach' or not, the more you learn about The city's cooking the more interesting and magical the square mile becomes. So let us begin our discrete little tour through the alleyways, along the streets with such peculiar names and into the hidden kitchens of the City of London, to see what we discover.

CHAPTER 1

THE SHERIFFS' BREAKFAST

The Sin of Gluttony *"Let it be said that of all the deadly sins that mankind may commit, the fifth appears to be the one that least troubles his conscience and causes him the least remorse."*
– *GRIMOD DE LAREYNIÉRE*

It is a rather appropriate start to this City cookbook that we begin with both the first meal of the day and the first appointed officers of the City of London. Since the 7th Century, long before any Mayoralty or council there was a Sheriff of London responsible for collecting taxes and imposing the King's justice. Since 1132 the citizens of the City have been granted the right to elect their own sheriff and in the late 19th Century this was increased to two. Remarkably, we still have two sheriffs today; among their responsibilities are overseeing the procedures at The Old Bailey, where they reside for their year of office and I am sure start each day with a good breakfast!

The Sheriffs' Breakfast itself is a major annual City event. It dates back over 500 years, when it was decreed that on Michaelmas Eve, (the day before St Michael the Archangel's feast day – 28th September – but you, of course, knew that) at 8 o'clock in the morning, the sheriff would be sworn in and then entertain the Alderman of the City at breakfast.

The oldest record of a City breakfast I can find is that of Samuel Pepys in about 1660, when the assembled company would have partaken in a sumptuous menu comprising such delicacies as *mutton pottage, turkey pie, goose, pickled oysters, collar of a brawn,* all washed down with ale and a *pot of chocolate.*

I therefore got quite excited when I was recently invited to cook the Sheriffs' Breakfast in one of the City's magnificent Livery Halls. I had visions of huge long tables laden with joints of gammon, cold partridge, pigeon and other fowl, potted beef, anchovies, sweet meats, cakes and huge jugs of beer and wine. But alas, in recent years, this particular breakfast has been translated into a rather grand formal luncheon – not a fried egg or slice of smoked bacon in sight.

Breakfast in the City of London in general, however, is very much still alive. The Power Breakfast, for example, is the occasion when extremely important business people, who could not possibly have time to dine together at a more user friendly time of day, meet to discuss major deals across *Eggs Benedict* or *Poached Kippers* – safe in the knowledge that no member of the financial press would possibly go out to eat at 7am. There is a wonderful occasion I cook for known as the Budget Breakfast – anything but 'budget' is the archetypal Power Breakfast, a sumptuous feast at which one of the world's largest firms of accountants entertain business magnets the morning after the Chancellor's Budget to expound interpretation and consequence of what has been announced.

Breakfast is, of course, not only served to start the day. Any self-respecting ball will serve breakfast in the middle of the night before guests find their 'carriages' home. There have been some spectacular Balls in the City – Lloyds are granted special permission to use the market streets and colonnades of Leadenhall for their biannual ball. Venetian Masked Balls are regular features in the magnificent Royal Exchange or Mansion House and themed charity balls in the Guildhall.

One of my own less glorious catering moments was cooking breakfast for a ball in a very exclusive private club that must remain nameless. I had been allowed to take over the club's kitchens for the night, presumably because their own chefs were unwilling to cook *Scrambled Eggs* for 600 at 3am. Now, whisking 1200 eggs is not as easy as you may think and I spotted a wonderful old Hobart Mixer the size of a large wheelbarrow, into which we poured our eggs. I cannot have looked away for more than a few seconds, but the next thing I saw was the massive bowl on its side and a sea of egg mix oozing slowly across the kitchen floor in every direction. (A lava of eggs may be less dangerous that molten rock but it is equally unstoppable.)

This was the moment that the club manager decided to visit his kitchens to ensure all was well. A rather officious man whose response to my shouts of "don't come through" was an instant "don't you tell me what to do" slipped flat on his back into the egg mix. The Ball survived and more eggs were brought from our depot but I have never to this day been invited back to the club.

Nowadays, many a City worker starts their day with a muesli bar, a smoothie or a cappuccino. A true British Breakfast however, is of course a fry-up, and around the outer edges of the City, particularly in Smithfield, Clerkenwell, Aldgate and Blackfriars, there are still places serving bacon, sausages, black pudding, tomatoes, mushrooms, fried bread, fried eggs and of course a mug of sweet tea. Bad for the cholesterol, but a great start to the working day!

"Only dull people are brilliant at breakfast" – OSCAR WILDE

EGGS BENEDICT

From the Great Eastern to Claridges, Eggs Benedict hold their position as the number one sophisticated Power Breakfast dish. The poached egg must be runny, the muffin crispy and the hollandaise just bubbling on top.

INGREDIENTS FOR 6

6 eggs
1 tsp. wine vinegar
3 english muffins
25g softened butter

6 slices of good quality ham
250ml hollandaise (chapter 15)
a few chopped chives to
  garnish

METHOD

- To poach the eggs, fill a wide saucepan with about 3 inches of water, bring gently to a simmer and then add the vinegar.
- Carefully break the eggs into the simmering water and allow to cook for $2\frac{1}{2}$–3 minutes – yolks should still be soft in the centre. Remove the eggs with a slotted spoon and keep to one side.
- While the eggs are poaching, cut the muffins in half, toast them under the grill and spread with butter
- Arrange the muffins on a baking tin then top each of them with a slice of ham, a poached egg and a spoon of hollandaise.
- Place under a hot grill until nicely browned. Sprinkle with the chopped chives and serve immediately.

KIPPER KEDGEREE

Kedgeree is one of those any-time dishes suitable for breakfast, lunch or supper. Here we are using kipper but almost any flaky-fleshed fish can be substituted, including salmon, halibut, cod and haddock. Make sure you re-moisten the kedgeree with the cooking liquor just before serving.

INGREDIENTS FOR 6–8

450g kipper fillets	175g long grain rice
parsley, bay leaf and pepper-corns	50g butter
	2 tbsp. parsley, chopped
600ml milk	freshly ground black pepper
2 eggs	150ml double cream (optional)
120g frozen peas	

METHOD

- Place the kippers in a deep roasting tin with a few sprigs of parsley, bay leaf and peppercorns, pour over the milk and cook in the oven at 200°C for 15–20 minutes.
- Whilst the fish is cooking, hard boil the eggs, cook and drain the peas and cook the rice in boiling salted water until soft.
- When the kippers are cooked, break the flesh into flakes and remove all bones. Reserve the liquid. Peel and chop the eggs.
- Melt the butter and stir together the fish, peas, rice, egg and chopped parsley. Check the seasoning – it is unlikely that you will want to add salt but a few good turns with the pepper mill will be important.
- Moisten with some of the reserved cooking liquid and/or double cream. The dish can be served immediately or reheated and re-moistened when required.

FRENCH TOAST WITH CRISPY PANCETTA
AND MAPLE SYRUP

If I mention Eggy Bread, everyone says "yummy, how delicious." It reminds us of our childhood and it is never a bad thing to remember that we were all carefree children once upon a time. So why not include it in the culinary repertoire of a City filled with busy adults who sometimes take themselves too seriously?

INGREDIENTS FOR 6

4 eggs

½ tsp. salt

freshly ground black pepper

300ml milk

60g butter

6 slices of bread

12 slices of pancetta

maple syrup to drizzle

METHOD

- Crack the eggs into a shallow dish, then whisk in the salt, pepper and milk.
- Dip each slice of bread in the egg mixture, turning each side.
- Melt the butter in a heavy non-stick frying pan and fry the slices of bread on each side until golden brown.
- Whilst frying the bread, grill the pancetta on both sides until crispy.
- Transfer the toasts onto a serving platter and top with the pancetta.
- Drizzle over maple syrup and serve immediately.

GORDON RAMSAY'S OMELETTE ARNOLD BENNETT

Created as an after-theatre supper for the renowned novelist and theatre critic, Arnold Bennett, this dish remains a popular choice at the Savoy Grill, particularly under the guidance of the talented Marcus Wareing. This recipe is an updated version of the original but is equally satisfying.

INGREDIENTS FOR 6

300g undyed smoked haddock
a few sprigs of thyme
2 bay leaves
1 tbsp. black peppercorns
1 shallot, peeled and sliced
300ml milk
225ml double cream
15 large eggs, plus 1 egg yolk

45g medium cheddar (or parmesan), finely grated
30g cold butter, cut into small pieces
sea salt and freshly ground black pepper
handful of flat leaf parsley, chopped

METHOD

- Place the haddock, thyme, bay leaves, peppercorns and shallot in a pan. Add the milk and top with enough cold water to cover then bring to a gentle simmer. Poach the fish for 2–3 minutes, remove with a slotted spoon and drain.
- Once cooked, flake the fish into bite-size pieces, discarding the skin and any bones.
- Strain the milk into a clean, wide saucepan. Bring to the boil and cook until the liquid has reduced by two thirds. Add the cream and simmer until thickened and reduce by another half.
- Mix the single egg yolk and grated cheese into the reduced cream.
- Melt a few knobs of butter in a non-stick omelette pan. Lightly beat the eggs, season with salt and pepper then pour into the pan and swirl the eggs around. Stir with a wooden spoon or fork and shake the pan frequently to evenly cook the eggs.
- When the eggs are two thirds set, remove the pan from the heat. Scatter the flaked haddock on top, spoon the cheese sauce over and place the pan under a very hot grill until the topping is golden brown.
- Slide the omelette onto a warm serving plate and garnish with a sprinkling of chopped parsley.

DEVILLED KIDNEYS IN BAKED BLACK MUSHROOMS

I don't wish to put you off, but it is reputed at the Old Bailey that kidneys were always served for breakfast on hanging days. This twist on traditional devilled kidneys created by Olivia Stewart-Cox takes a classic dish to a new level. The succulent spiced kidneys are perfectly complimented by the mushroom.

INGREDIENTS FOR 6
6 lamb's kidneys
6 large black flat mushrooms
50g butter
3 finely diced shallots
100ml white wine
100ml double cream
1 tbsp. of anchovy essence
chopped parsley and paprika
  to decorate

FOR MARINADE
2 tbsp. Worcester sauce
2 tbsp. sherry vinegar
1 tbsp. of tomato puree
1 tbsp. of English mustard
  powder
1 clove garlic
1 bay leaf a pinch of cayenne
  pepper
salt and pepper

METHOD
- Skin, core and half the kidneys.
- Mix up all the ingredients for the marinade, pour over the kidneys and leave to infuse for 8 hours or more.
- Place black flat mushrooms on a baking tray, remove stalks and paint with half of the butter. Bake at 180°C for 10 minutes.
- Remove the kidneys from the marinade and reserve.
- In a skillet, melt the remaining butter and add the shallots. Cook until soft.
- Now add in the kidneys and cook for 2–3 minutes on each side. Remove from pan, slice lengthways into 2, then place on to the cooked mushrooms and keep warm.
- Pour the marinade back into the pan and add white wine, cream, anchovy essence then boil for 2–3 minutes to reduce down to a coating consistency.
- Spoon the sauce over the kidneys and mushrooms and sprinkle generously with the chopped parsley and paprika.

CHAPTER 2

COFFEE HOUSE BUSINESS

Coffee is said to have first been eaten by sheep in Abyssinia who then spent 'an elated and sleepless night' on their hilltop; so the shepherds tried it themselves. It quickly became popular and after roasting, grinding and brewing in hot water turned out to be the perfect stimulant for keeping worshippers awake during their devotions in the Mosques. Coffee first came to Europe in the mid 17th Century and was variably described as 'most useless, since it serves neither for nourishment nor for debauchery' or as a 'pitiful drink – enough to bewitch a man and render him no use to women'. However, the fashion for drinking coffee quickly spread and 300 years later it is the world's most popular beverage, consumed from dawn to late at night in every conceivable café, bar, restaurant, home, workplace or institution. The coffee industry worldwide employs more than 25 million people – second only in world trade to oil.

The first coffee house to appear in the City of London opened in 1652 in St Michael's Alley, Cornhill. No, it was not a Starbucks, nor were they serving Mocha Lattes, Vanilla Macchiatos or Hazelnut Cappuccinos, but nonetheless, the craze for coffee had begun. Today there is a coffee shop on most street corners and we have counted exactly one hundred within the square mile. Now you may think these institutions are just innocent places of refreshment and recreation – where secretaries meet their friends to gossip about office politics and make-up, or where illicit lovers rendezvous to whisper together and hold hands beneath their Café Americanos and Espressos. Little would you imagine that syndicates may be forming to dominate the world's stock markets or high-powered negotiation may be underway to agree terms for marine reinsurance.

Back in 1698, however, some of the City's most important financial institutions were forming over a dish or two of the aromatic brown brew. Stock brokers and stock jobbers carried out their trade doing informal deals in coffee shops along Change Alley. Most notable of these was Jonathan Castaing who issued a twice-weekly list of stock and commodity prices called 'The Course of the Exchange and Other Things'. Here is an extract from it:

London, Tuesday 4ᵗʰ January, 1698.

	Advanced	Paid Off
Tobacco	1500000	119400
Poll Tax	569293	479328
Salt Act	1904519	73772
Low Wines	69959	11100
Coal Act & Leath	564700	17162
Malt Act	200000	163745

By John Castaing, Broker, at his Office at Jonathan's Coffee house.

Jonathan's Coffee House was the first formal base of stock dealings and as the business developed it became known as New Jonathan's in Sweeting Alley then changed its name to The Stock Exchange. Thus emerged one of the most important financial institutions in the world.

Edward Lloyd had his coffee house in Lombard Street where he encouraged a clientele of ship owners, captains, wealthy merchants and brokers so they could arrange insurance cover for their cargoes and vessels. Again, this establishment moved around the City, each time improving in status right up to the new Lloyds building at One Lime Street which still today dominates the international insurance market.

The original coffee houses were not just about business. For a penny admission charge, they provided a convivial place for like-minded people to discuss politics and literature, hear news and gamble. Whilst City houses were the forerunners of financial institutions, such places as Whites in St James were the forerunners of the gentleman's club. Sadly, however, I can find no record of any food being consumed in these places. Drinks were extended to 'Tea' – a beverage from northern China and 'Chocolate' described as 'more a drink for pigs than a drink for humanity' but not even a Twix or a doughnut seem to have been on offer. How then can I provide recipes to compliment the City of London's coffee house heritage? There follows a selection of both savoury and sweet little somethings that I hope will enhance your own 'elated and sleepless' sessions of drinking coffee.

CHEESE STRAWS WITH PAPRIKA, SESAME OR POPPY SEEDS

There is something very English about cheese straws and you can eat them at almost any time – a mid-morning snack, a canapé, a savoury or a garnish for starters.

INGREDIENTS FOR 24

110g plain flour
salt, pepper, cayenne pepper
75g butter, chilled
1 egg yolk
110g cheddar cheese, grated

paprika
sesame seeds
poppy seeds
a little milk

METHOD

- Put the flour, salt, pepper and a pinch of cayenne together in a bowl. Grate in the butter, add the cheese and combine with your hands to form 'breadcrumbs.'
- Turn out onto a floured surface, make a well, add the egg yolk and knead into a ball.
- Roll out the dough and cut into strips 10cm long, 1cm wide and ½cm thick.
- Space the straws well apart on a baking tray lined with baking paper.
- Brush the cheese straws with milk. Sprinkle some with paprika, some with sesame and the remainder with poppy seeds.
- Bake in the oven at 200°C for 10–15 minutes until golden brown.

ROSEMARY SCONES

Bakers will always cook in batches of 13: 12 to sell and one for him or her to sample. The key tip to making scones is don't overwork the dough or it becomes chewy.

INGREDIENTS FOR A BAKER'S DOZEN

450g plain flour
15g salt
5 tsp. baking powder
115g butter
225g grated cheddar

275ml milk
1 large sprig of fresh rosemary
    taken off the stalk and finely
    chopped

METHOD

- Place the flour, salt and baking powder into a bowl. Rub in the butter to make 'breadcrumbs' and then add 200g of the grated cheese.
- Make a well in the centre, pour in the milk stirring to combine.
- Turn on to a floured surface, pat together and roll to 1–1½ inches thick then stamp out into rounds using a 2″ cutter.
- Top each scone with the remaining grated cheese and chopped rosemary
- Place well apart on a baking sheet lined with baking paper.
  Bake in a 200°C oven for 10–15 minutes until risen and golden brown.

ANTONY WORALL THOMPSON'S SMOKED SALMON AND CRAB PARCELS

Delicious little crab and apple morsels that cry out for that mid-morning glass of Taittinger – sorry, I forgot we were on coffee.

INGREDIENTS FOR 24 PARCELS

24 x 15g slices of smoked
  salmon
3 tbsp. sour cream
2 tbsp. mayonnaise
1 tbsp. horseradish
4 spring onions, finely sliced
2 tsp. mint, chopped

1 cox's apple, peeled, cored
  and diced
1 medium hot green pepper,
  finely chopped
1 lemon, zested, juice of ½
250g fresh white crabmeat
salt and pepper

METHOD

- In a bowl, mix the sour cream, mayonnaise and horseradish, then add all the other ingredients except the smoked salmon. Season with salt and pepper.
- Lay each slice of smoked salmon on a piece of lightly oiled clingfilm twice the size of the salmon.
- Top each slice with a teaspoon of the crab mix. Pull the cling film up around the salmon and twist the top making a shape like a small inverted bowl.
- Refrigerate to set. Remove from the fridge half an hour before you wish to serve. Unwrap just before serving.

ANCHOVY AND BASIL CAMEL'S FEET

I have a wonderful story of a great City old boy asking: "Mr Gladwin is this camel you are serving us?" I won't say more but he was not referring to this dish which is simply an anchovy and pesto pastry rolled into the shape of a camel's footprint.

INGREDIENTS FOR 24
1 pkt. ready rolled puff pastry
2 tbsp. pesto
1 small tin anchovy fillets
2 tbsp. grated parmesan
salt and pepper

METHOD
- Unroll the puff pastry onto a baking sheet and spread with pesto right to the sides on the short edges but leaving 2cm spare on the long edge.
- Lay the anchovy fillets out lengthways all over the pastry. Sprinkle with parmesan.
- Brush the long edges with a little water and then roll them both inwards so that they meet and stick in the middle. Chill for 30 minutes.
- Cut the chilled roll into ½ cm slices and place them flat and well spaced on a baking sheet lined with baking paper. Cook in the oven at 200°C for 10–15 minutes until golden brown.

MINIATURE CRUMPETS
WITH THREE FLAVOUR BUTTERS

There is nothing like a bit of crumpet and I promise home cooking makes them twice as delicious. The only tricky point is spooning the batter into a metal ring on the frying pan – beware.

INGREDIENTS FOR APPROXIMATELY 24 MINIS

375ml warm water	For butters
1 dstsp. dried yeast	100g salted butter
1 tsp. castor sugar	1 tbsp. mixed fresh herbs,
225g plain flour	chopped
½ tbsp. baking powder	1 tbsp. sunblushed
½ tsp. salt	tomatoes,chopped
½ tsp. mixed spice	Marmite

METHOD

- Mix the warm water, dried yeast and sugar together in a bowl and leave in a warm place for 10 minutes until the yeast activates and starts to rise.
- Sift the flour, baking powder, salt and mixed spice into a bowl, mix in the yeast and leave to rise again for 30–40 minutes so the batter becomes light and fluffy.
- To cook the crumpets, carefully grease the insides of some small metal rings and arrange them in a non-stick frying pan over a medium heat. When hot, spoon a teaspoon of the mixture into each ring. Cook for 4–6 minutes, tiny bubbles will appear and then burst.
- Re-grease the rings before using again.
- Soften the butter and divide into three pots. Add the mixed herbs to one pot, the sunblushed tomatoes to the second and Marmite, to taste, to the third.
- Spread the crumpets generously with the butters and flash under the grill until the butter starts to melt.

ROSEWATER SHORTBREAD

Deliciously scented biscuits ideal for entertaining elderly relatives or the vicar to elevenses or afternoon tea.

INGREDIENTS FOR 12 PIECES
250g unsalted butter
60g castor sugar
8–10 drops rosewater
250g plain flour
25g cornflour

METHOD
* Soften the butter, sugar and rosewater and mix with a wooden spoon until well combined.
* Add the flour and cornflour and work the ingredients together – finishing with your hands until it forms a soft dough.
* Roll out on a floured board to 6mm (¼ inch) thick, cut out discs with a pastry cutter.
* Dust with castor sugar.
* Place on a baking sheet lined with baking paper and bake in the oven at 170°C for about 20–30 minutes until golden brown.

CHOCOLATE AND PISTACHIO BROWNIES

Brownies should be crisp on the outside, moist in the middle, incredibly bad for your waistline and truly irresistible.

INGREDIENTS FOR 12

255g dark chocolate
255g butter
1 tsp. vanilla essence
280g soft brown sugar
280g castor sugar

5 eggs, beaten
280g plain flour
2 tsp. baking powder
½tsp. salt
80g pistachio nuts, peeled

METHOD

- In a heavy-based saucepan gently melt the chocolate, butter and vanilla essence over a low heat, then add both sugars and melt again.
- Transfer to a large bowl and stir in the beaten eggs. Sift the flour, baking powder and salt and fold these in.
- Finally, add in the pistachio nuts, then pour the mixture into an oiled and lined cake tin.
- Cook in the oven at 170°C for 30 minutes.
- Cool then cut into neat fingers or diamonds.

MARZIPAN BUMBLEBEES

A few hundred years ago, marzipan was the great dessert speciality and no banquet was complete without it. Why not then these small bumblebees?

INGREDIENTS FOR 24
300g ground almonds
150g castor sugar
150g icing sugar
1 egg, beaten
¼ tsp. almond extract
50g dark chocolate

METHOD
- Mix the almonds, sugar and icing sugar together in a bowl. Add the egg and almond extract. Knead the marzipan into a smooth ball and then roll out to form a long oval sausage.
- Cut into lozenges no more than ½cm thick.
- Melt the chocolate in a bowl above a pan of simmering water. Half dip the marzipan into the chocolate and leave to set on a tray lined with greaseproof paper.
- Store in an airtight container and serve any-time.

PEPPERMINT CREAMS

This is one of those childhood treats that I promise will bring memories flooding back.

INGREDIENTS
1 egg white
225g icing sugar
1 tsp. peppermint essence
a few drops of green food colouring

METHOD
- In a large bowl whisk the egg white until it is frothy but not stiff.
- Sift the icing sugar into a large bowl and add the egg white, peppermint essence and food colouring.
- Knead together with your hands until the colour is evenly distributed then roll into a sausage shape and cut into lozenges.
- Place on a lined tray and leave to dry overnight.

Jonathan's Coffee House

BRANDY SNAPS

Professional kitchens are constantly required to make brandy snaps. They are used as biscuits, petit fours, containers for ice creams or garnishes for elaborate desserts of all kinds. We have tried most recipes and this equal quantities of all 4 ingredients is not only the easiest to remember but the easiest to get right.

INGREDIENTS
75g butter
75g castor sugar
75g golden syrup
75g plain flour

METHOD
- Place the butter, sugar and golden syrup in a small heavy-based saucepan and melt gently, stirring all the time.
- Add the flour and stir to form a stiff paste. Pour into a bowl and leave to get completely cold.
- Roll teaspoon sized balls of the mixture and place them well apart on a baking sheet lined with baking paper. Cook a few at a time in the oven at 200°C for 8–10 minutes until golden brown.
- Remove from the oven and allow to set for just one minute. Whilst still soft, carefully lift off each biscuit with a palette knife and mould into shape.
- To make traditional brandy snaps, wrap them around the handle of a wooden spoon, for a curl wrap around a rolling pin or to make a basket wrap over a plum or orange.

CHAPTER 3

A PRESIDENT TO LUNCH

"I drink it when I am happy, and when I am sad. Sometimes I drink it when I am alone. When I have company I consider it obligatory. I trifle with it if I am not hungry, and drink it when I am. Otherwise I never touch it – unless I am thirsty." – MADAME LILY BOLLINGER

In America, those in the corporate world who don't make Presidents are all Vice Presidents and if not that, aspiring assistants to Vice Presidents. And in The City of London, in spite of all the tradition and heritage, there is a big American invasion force including plenty of American bosses – so it is not that unusual to entertain a President to lunch.

From the hidden sanctum of a restaurant kitchen, you can always spot them from the order coming in. 'Sauce on the side' is one of the first give-aways. It means, 'I am not sure I am going to like your sauce but I don't want to miss out so I'll have some anyway'. Another is the inevitable 'send back' of crustaceans in shell, fish on the bone or poultry with carcasses. Except for a few quick strokes with a sharp steak knife, food for a President should apparently be eaten with only a fork and minimum effort. Finally, there is the 'plain lobster, green salad, no dressing' and the 'I just got in from across the pond, can't you just make an omelette' or a variety of other requests for items not on the menu.

Other countries, of course, have Presidents too and when a foreign Head of State visits London, the Corporation of the City plays a major role in entertaining him or her. Britain in general and the City in particular are masters of the pomp and ceremony required to present a major State Banquet and I have had the privilege to cook for several such splendid occasions held in the Guildhall.

All state visits follow a particular protocol and on the first day the president or monarch dines with the Queen at Buckingham Palace. The following day, he or she dines with 'the people' at an event hosted by the Lord Mayor. This is the opportunity to meet a fairly exclusive range of the great and the good in the City. Naturally, the Queen's choice of menu takes priority. There is then liaison with the Embassy on the likes and dislikes of the visiting big wig and finally a committee of tasters is appointed to select the perfect menu and wines.

One such memorable occasion was a visit by the President of Italy. This particular President was extremely old and it was decided lunch would be more appropriate than dinner (you cannot have your guest of honour dropping off during the speeches). The instructions for lunch were also very clear – he would only drink Italian wine, preferably accompanied by some classic Italian food. The Corporation could just about cope with the first but spaghetti was out of the question! It was then discovered that all this wonderful modern, British cooking we are so proud of, riddled with balsamic, olive oil, pancetta, sweet basil and so many more – perhaps had something to do with Italy and this request for Italian friendly food might not be so difficult after all.

At a magnificent tasting session of twelve Anglo-Italian dishes matched to a dozen different Italian wines, we selected a Wild Mushroom and Herb Salad with Redcurrants. Followed by Roasted Fillet of Black Bream with Minted Pea Puree, Seared Lemon and Thyme Dressing. Finished off with miniature White Port Soufflé, Caramelised Oranges and Plums.

The influence of Italian cooking even extends to our politicians. David Cameron was kind enough to submit a recipe for spicy Italian sausages with tomatoes, double cream and pasta that I could not quite fit in. But here are some light continental starter dishes fit for a President or even possibly a future Prime Minister.

"Everything you see I owe to spaghetti." – SOPHIA LOREN

CHARGRILLED ASPARAGUS, AUBERGINE, TOMATO WITH MOZZARELLA, BALSAMIC REDUCTION

A very stylish vegetable and mozzarella stack dressed up with Balsamic Reduction and a sprinkle of paprika. You will need a good quality ribbed griddle pan to achieve effective chargrilling.

INGREDIENTS FOR 6

18 sticks asparagus
1 medium aubergine
3 ripe plum tomatoes
2 buffalo mozzarella
fresh thyme

extra virgin olive oil
salt and black pepper
balsamic reduction (see
   chapter 15)

METHOD

- Trim the ends of the asparagus, slice the aubergine into 12 and cut each tomato length into 4.
- Brush all the vegetables with olive oil and season with Maldon salt and freshly ground pepper.
- Slice the mozzarella and marinate in olive oil with chopped thyme, salt and pepper.
- Heat a ribbed griddle pan to very hot then chargrill first the asparagus, then the aubergine then very briefly the tomato slices until cooked and tender.
- Arrange 3 asparagus spears on each plate and top with alternating slices of aubergine, tomato and mozzarella to form a stack.
- Drizzle the balsamic reduction around the edge and sprinkle with paprika.

WARM MUSHROOM SALAD WITH GOATS CHEESE CROSTINI

I find warm mushroom salads irresistible. It is something to do with my bohemian Russian mother foraging in the woods for the perfect Cèpe and then just frying it in butter and serving on toast for tea. The key is very light cooking and serving instantly. Here, the contrast of crunchy goats cheese crostini compliments the mushrooms beautifully.

INGREDIENTS FOR 6
9 thin slices of French bread
150g goats cheese
250g mixed wild mushrooms,sliced
125g button mushrooms, cut into quarters
125g black flat mushrooms,sliced
1 bag mixed leaf salad

FOR THE DRESSING
4 tbsp. balsamic vinegar
2 tbsp. soft brown sugar
1 tbsp. Dijon mustard
salt and pepper
250ml olive oil
2 tbsp. walnut oil

METHOD
- Cut the French bread slices in halves, dip in olive oil, lay out in a tin and bake in the oven until golden brown.
- When the crostini are cooked, crumble goats cheese on the top of each one and grill to melt the cheese. Keep warm.
- Mix the vinegar, sugar, mustard, salt and pepper together then whisk in the olive and walnut oil.
- Dress the salad with half of the vinaigrette and divide the salad between six plates.
- Pour the remaining dressing into a heavy-bottomed frying pan and heat until sizzling. Add the mushrooms and toss briefly until lightly cooked, warm and coated in dressing. Spoon over the salad and top with 3 warm crostini per person.

TERENCE CONRAN'S CROUSTADE OF QUAIL'S EGGS WITH MUSHROOM DUXELLE AND SAUCE HOLLANDAISE

The challenge to this recipe will be the peeling of the quail eggs. I have in the past set my kitchen team to peel 1500 and it did not go down well. A soft boiled quail egg however, is a truly delicious thing and this delightful starter from Terence Conran's lovely restaurant in the Royal Exchange will be well worth the effort.

INGREDIENTS FOR 6

1 pkt. ready rolled puff pastry
1 egg, beaten
30 quail's eggs
55g butter
500g field mushrooms, finely chopped
1 clove garlic

1 tbsp. Madeira
salt and pepper
¼tsp. thyme leaves
200ml sauce hollandaise (see chapter 15)
chervil to garnish

METHOD

- Cut the pastry into 6 discs and lightly score a circle inside half a cm from the edge.
- Place on a baking sheet lined with baking paper, brush with beaten egg and bake in the oven at 200°C for 15–20 minutes, until golden and puffed.
- Allow to cool and then cut out the inner circle. Remove and discard the excess pastry.
- Bring a large pan of water to the boil and gently place the quail's eggs in. Cook for 2½ minutes and then drain and plunge into ice-cold water. Peel the eggs and chill until needed.
- For the Duxelles, sweat the garlic and mushrooms in a pan over a low heat. Add the Madeira and allow to reduce.
- Cool the mushrooms and when cold place in a tea towel and squeeze out any excess moisture. Add the thyme and season with salt and pepper.
- To serve, fill the puff pastry case with a tablespoon of the mushroom duxelle, place 5 quail's eggs in each one. Spoon over some hollandaise and heat in the oven at 200°C for 5–10 minutes. Decorate with a chervil sprig.

HONEY POACHED BLACK FIGS WITH PARMA HAM

There is nothing better than lunching under an Italian olive tree eating Parma ham with delicious ripe fresh figs. Here in the City, however, you may well have a miniature olive tree on your balcony, the purchase of good San Daniele ham is possible, but all too often the figs we buy are dry and flavourless. This is a recipe for perfect figs every time.

INGREDIENTS FOR 6
12 large black figs
12 slices parma ham
1 bag of rocket
1 cinnamon stick
2 cloves
2 star anise
salt and freshly ground black
  pepper

FOR THE SAVOURY SYRUP
3 tbsp. honey
2 tbsp. balsamic vinegar
300ml water
200ml white wine

METHOD
- Place all the ingredients for the syrup into a saucepan, season well with salt and ground black pepper and bring to the boil. Reduce by about half the quantity to make a shiny glaze.
- Snip the tips off the figs and place in a small shallow tin.
- Spoon the syrup over the figs and bake for 15–20 minutes at 180°C until soft but not flabby.
- Remove from the oven and leave to cool.
- Arrange the rocket and parma ham on a platter and finish with roasted figs topped with the remaining syrup.

CRISPY MONEYBAGS OF SMOKED TROUT
AND HORSERADISH

You can imagine why a dish named moneybags is popular in the City. These delightfully simple crispy parcels are the ideal 'softening up' dish to prepare before discussing with your partner the overdraft, overpriced or overspend.

INGREDIENTS
3 250g fillets of smoked trout
250g cream cheese
2 tbs. horseradish relish
juice of ½ lemon
cracked black pepper
1 pack filo pastry

TO ACCOMPANY
mixed leaves
lemon wedges
crème fraîche
a little melted butter

METHOD
- In a mixing bowl, combine the cream cheese and smoked trout with a fork.
- Stir in the horseradish relish, lemon juice and black pepper.
- Lay the filo pastry out on a work surface and cut into 10cm squares. Then place one square on top of another at an angle to form an eight-pointed star.
- Place a dessert spoonful of the smoked trout filling in the middle of the filo. Wet round the edge with a pastry brush, gather up the edge and pinch together to form a little money bag.
- Place on a lined baking tray and paint with melted butter. Bake at 200°C for 6–8 minutes until golden brown.
- Serve warm with a little leaf salad, wedges of lemon and crème fraîche

CHAPTER 4

TUPPENCE A BAG

Was the street vendor in Mary Poppins who sold breadcrumbs at tuppence a bag as near as I am going to get to a culinary reference for St Paul's? I have actually cooked a meal in the great cathedral – not in the refectory or café, but in the main crypt directly beneath the altar. It was at the time when International Corporations in the City of London were competing with one another by luring clients with ever more lavish and unusual hospitality. This particular organisation was sponsoring a classical concert in the cathedral and I imagine, by means of suitable donation, had one-off permission to entertain 250 of their VIP guests to dinner in the crypt afterwards.

St Paul's from St Martins le Grand

The installation of mobile cookers, tables, chairs, catering equipment etc was all carried out well before the concert. What had not been mentioned, perhaps not even thought of, however, was that there are open iron grates in the stone slabs of St Paul's nave and once the orchestra began to play, every note was audible to us below. And vice versa? We quickly found out the slightest clink of glassware or tinkle of cutlery would be heard above. Imagine a team of 40 catering staff tiptoeing about trying to soundlessly lay 250 extravagant place settings and assembling 250 elaborate first course plates. The situation became farcical with our attempts to pause stock still when the music halted and then carrying out frantic activity to keep up with the symphony's crescendos. Half of us got the giggles and had to go outside to recover. In the end there were no major crashes, the dinner was well received and I had no reports of a new percussion accompaniment to Handel's Messiah.

For 300 years St Paul's has been the very centre of London. Even with competition from the Millennium Wheel or the Gherkin, Christopher Wren's masterpiece continues to dominate the skyline of the City. Alas, however, my research efforts to relate the great cathedral to cooking have revealed precious little except for references to gruel. The mighty workforce of stonemasons, carpenters, tilers and glaziers who worked on the building for 35 years from 1675 until 1710 were apparently sustained with a variety of pottages and gruels from mutton, onion, bean,pig, barley or oatmeal to the Sunday special 'water gruel.' I think we might content ourselves with the spiritual nourishment St Paul's undoubtedly supplies to the City. Here are some wonderful 'graces' said as the prelude to give thanks before good eating and there follows a set of suitably humble soup recipes good for the soul.

GOOD GRACES

Canon David Meara, Rector of St Brides, Fleet Street
Bless us Lord and Bless our food
And keep us in a merry mood
Bless the cooks and all who serve us
From indigestion Lord preserve us. **Amen.**

Mr Eric Burns
God give us grace... so in this race
There isn't just one winner.
But fat or thin... we all can win
And share this lovely dinner. **Amen.**

Bishop Charles Gore
Lord, Forgive us that we eat while others starve. **Amen.**

Robert Burns
Some hae meat, and canna eat,
And some wad eat that want it,
But we hae meat and we can eat,
And sae the Lord be thank it. **Amen.**

Robert Herrick
God! To my little meal and oil
Add but a bit of flesh to boil
And thou my pipkinnet shalt see
Give a wave-offering to thee. **Amen.**

WATERCRESS AND ALMOND SOUP

Susie Robinson's lovely pale green soup combining the fresh peppery taste of watercress with the nutty body of ground almonds is a sure-fire winner. Susie created it when she and I first started Party Ingredients Private Catering and we still get regular requests for both the dish and the recipe 30 years on.

INGREDIENTS FOR 6

15g butter	100g ground almonds
225g potatoes, diced	600ml chicken stock
2 bunches watercress	600ml milk
grated rind of 1 lemon	salt and pepper

METHOD

- Melt the butter in a large saucepan and toss the potatoes, one bunch of watercress, lemon rind and almonds in it for about 1 minute.
- Add the stock and milk. Bring to the boil and simmer for 20 minutes. When the potatoes are cooked, puree in a food processor until smooth. Alternatively, use a mouli-grinder. Add salt and pepper to taste.
- The soup can now be left and reheated when needed. Just before serving, chop the remaining bunch of watercress finely and add to the soup to finish.

"The qualities of an exceptional cook are akin to those of a successful tightrope walker: an abiding passion for the task, courage to go out on a limb and an impeccable sense of balance."
– BRYAN MILLER

TERENCE CONRAN'S CLASSIC FISH SOUP

A good fish soup, French bread croutons, grated cheese and several bottles of good rough red stuff is the perfect recipe for a lazy all afternoon session. There is quite a bit of work in preparing the soup but it will be well worth it.

INGREDIENTS FOR 6–8
150ml olive oil
1 onion, finely chopped
1 leek, finely chopped
2 fennel, finely chopped
3 cloves of garlic, finely chopped
4 bay leaves
1 small piece orange peel
6 tomatoes, blanched, peeled, roughly chopped
1.5kg variety of fish e.g. red mullet, haddock, hake or bream
2 litres water
a pinch of saffron
1 crab

ROUILLE
2 large red peppers, cored, de-seeded and cut into quarters
1 slice of thick bread, crusts removed
3 cloves of garlic, peeled
1 large mild red chilli
1 egg yolk
¼tsp. salt and pepper
100ml olive oil
500g mussels and clams, cleaned
salt and pepper

METHOD
- Heat the olive oil in a large heavy-bottomed saucepan, add the vegetables, garlic, bay leaves and orange peel and cook to soften. Add the tomatoes and stew for a further 10 minutes.
- Chop the fish into large pieces and add to the pot along with 2 litres of boiling water and the saffron.
- Exercising great care – kill the crab! Roughly chop it up and add the whole thing to the pot.
- Simmer gently for 40 minutes, removing any foam from the surface.
- Pound the fish and push it through a mouli-grinder then a sieve along with all the liquid.

- Return the soup to a large pan, add the clams and mussels and allow to come to the boil. Again remove any foam from the top and season with salt and freshly ground black pepper.

METHOD FOR ROUILLE
- Place the peppers on a hot grill until the skin blackens.
- Having removed all trace of the skin, place the peppers in a large pestle and mortar along with the bread, garlic, chilli, egg yolk, salt and pepper.
- Pound methodically to a smooth paste. Then add the olive oil drop by drop.
- Serve the soup with a large pot of Rouille, French Bread Croutons and grated parmesan.

ROASTED BUTTERNUT SOUP

One of my absolute favourites. The rich, mellow flavour of butternut squash spiced with black pepper needs very little added to it, just ensure you buy or make a good quality vegetable stock with no unwanted additives.

INGREDIENTS FOR 6

1½kg butternut squash
3 tbsp. olive oil salt and
    freshly ground black pepper
2 onions, finely chopped

150ml vegetable stock
750ml milk
1 tbsp. pumpkin seeds, toasted

METHOD
- Peel and halve the squash, scooping out all the seeds then cut into 3 inch chunks.
- Coat the squash with 1 tbsp. of olive oil, salt and lots of ground black pepper then roast in a 200°C oven for 20 minutes until soft and caramelised.
- Meanwhile, heat the remaining olive oil in a large pan and cook the onions gently for 10–15 minutes.
- Add the squash, stock and milk then bring to the boil.
- Simmer for a further 5 minutes until the squash begins to break up.Transfer the soup to a liquidiser and blend until smooth.
- Serve the soup piping hot, sprinkled with toasted pumpkin seeds. The rosemary scones in Chapter 2 will be ideal with it.

PHEASANT POACHER'S SOUP WITH PEARL BARLEY

I suppose you could buy a pheasant or use that scrawny old one in the bottom of your freezer, but it will not taste quite the same as if you sneak out into the countryside and poach one yourself. Either way, this rustic wholesome soup will certainly feed and nourish the family on a cold winter's night.

INGREDIENTS FOR 6

25g lard
1 large pheasant
6 bacon rashers
1 onion, chopped
2 old carrots, chopped
50g plain flour
1.75 litres cold water

75ml medium sherry
1 tbsp. brown sugar
1 tbsp. lemon juice
100g pearl barley
salt and freshly ground pepper
fresh chervil leaves

METHOD

- Set the oven at 220°C.
- Put the lard and pheasant in a roasting tin. Lay the bacon rashers over the bird and roast in the oven for 45 minutes.
- Once out of the oven and cool enough to handle, remove the bacon, chop it into small pieces and keep to one side. Lift the pheasant out of the tin and carefully scrape all the dripping into a large saucepan. Carve the flesh off the bird, save the bones and cut the meat into small strips. Add the meat to the bacon.
- Heat the saucepan of dripping and cook the pheasant bones, giblets, onion and carrots. Brown this mixture for a good 10 minutes, stirring occasionally. Now stir in the flour and cook for a further 3–4 minutes until it is well cooked but not burnt. Add all the water. Stirwell, then leave on a low heat to simmer for 1½–2 hours.
- Sieve the mixture to remove the bones and vegetables, then return the liquid to a clean saucepan. Add the sherry, brown sugar, lemon juice, pearl barley, salt and pepper and cook for a further 40 minutes, stirring occasionally.
- Finally, add the pheasant meat and bacon. Serve the soup with a sprinkling of chervil leaves.

GORDON RAMSAY'S LONDON PARTICULAR

We were thrilled with Mr Ramsay's recipe that could not be more 'City of London'. This soup is named after the old London 'Pea Soup' fogs from a time before environmental consciousness made us ban coal fires and gastronomic consciousness gave us Gordon.

INGREDIENTS FOR 6 PERSONS

375g dried split green peas	a few sprigs of thyme
3 tbsp. olive oil	1 bay leaf
1 large onion, peeled and chopped	375g smoked ham
	1½ litres water
1 stick of celery, trimmed and chopped	sea salt and freshly ground black pepper

METHOD

- Cover the dried split peas in cold water and leave to soak overnight.
- The next day, heat the olive oil in a heavy-based pot over medium heat. Stir in the onions, celery and herbs and cook for 5–6 minutes until the onions and celery are soft.
- Rinse and drain the peas thoroughly. Add to the pot and stir well. Nestle the ham among the peas and vegetables, then pour in enough water to cover. Bring the liquid to the boil and simmer. Skim off any froth that rises to the surface of the liquid. Slowly cook the soup for about 2–2½ hours until the peas are soft.
- Remove the ham from the soup and cut into small cubes. Whiz the soup in a blender in batches to a desired consistency. (I prefer mine to be a little chunky so I only process two thirds of the soup, then mix the puree with the remainder.) Add a little water if the overall soup is too thick. Taste and adjust the seasoning with salt and pepper.
- Return the ham pieces to the soup, reheat and serve hot.

CHAPTER 5

ROAST SWAN AND FINE CLARET

> *"I did not say that this meat was tough I just said I didn't see the horse that usually stands outside." – W.C FIELDS.*

As we have already established, the livery companies of the City of London are well known for their splendid "Halls" and lavish entertaining. There is, however, much more to them than multi-course banquets with vintage wines:–

Each livery represents a trade or craft and takes responsibility for the well being and development of its heritage. Many run education trusts, charities and alms houses, and some have obscure duties granted to them by Royal Charter, such as looking after the swans on the River Thames.

Both The Vintners' Company and The Dyers' Company celebrate their ancient right to nurture and eat swan with an annual Swan Feast Before I go on, however, be reassured that neither of these livery companies still actually serve swan. Chefs and caterers are sworn to secrecy about the use of a suitable substitute.

Only 20 years or so ago, one of the Vintners' Company Swan Uppers (a man employed to care for swans on the river) still used to provide me with swans to prepare. He would arrive at our kitchen door with a knotted dustbin bag containing one or two unfortunate young cygnets who had collided with overhead electricity cables, or met with some similar accident. We were obliged to pluck, draw and roast the birds, then strip off the flesh to use as an authentic contribution to the dish on the feast day. The swans themselves would cook away a remarkable amount of fat leaving some dark, rather sinewy, delicately spiced meat, indistinguishable from an undernourished goose.

At the Feast itself, to the herald of trumpets, a fully feathered stuffed swan is paraded by the chef into the banquet and presented to the Master with the words "for the delectation of your guests". Thereafter the "Swan" dish would be served as one of six courses in the guise of something like a Warm Swan Salad with Woodland

Mushrooms, Crispy Cygnet Parcels with Quince and Thyme, or Swan and Chestnut Croustade with Red Berry Chutney.

The Dyers' Company holds a very similar banquet and ceremony, but with the addition of a "Swan Song" – sung by a young tenor at the entrance of the parade. At a very recent Swan Feast, the newly elected Master Dyer announced that in the 40 years it had taken him to reach his eminent position, he had always wanted to sing this song himself.

Guests, liverymen and catering staff all cringed together at this prospect (and believe me even at such distinguished occasions, embarrassments of this kind can from time to time occur). To universal relief, however, the whole gathering was invited to sing together, forcefully led by the opera singer and to the great delight of all. I even hummed along myself whilst parading my stuffed bird.

Now, no self-respecting gentleman of the City would partake in eating swan without washing it down with a liberal amount of fine Bordeaux wine. The Vintners' Company (who, as you might imagine, are experts in such matters and can boast one of the finest red wine cellars in the world), have on some occasions found it necessary to serve two different First Growth "Cru Classe" Clarets – for the purpose of comparing vintages of course! I think delicate meat-based starters and salads using duck, goose, quail or offal etc. are absolutely delicious and far too rarely served with or without fine Claret. The final line of the swan presentation is "Pray Let the Cygnets be Served", so here are some recipe ideas:

DUCK CONFIT AND CRANBERRY PARCELS WITH SPICED BROCCOLI PUREE

Confit duck is one of those indulgent melt-in-the mouth things that is probably easier to buy than to make. However, for the purists, I have given a method, for the pragmatists, just buy a tin at any high quality food store. The substance of the spring roll wraps and the accompaniment of broccoli puree means this dish can happily be used as a main course:– Allow three parcels per person and serve a few new potatoes on the side.

INGREDIENTS FOR 6
4 duck legs
50g coarse sea salt
800g duck fat
40g dried cranberries
salt and pepper
12 spring roll wrappers or
  1 pack filo
20g melted butter

FOR THE PUREE
450g broccoli cut into florets
25g butter
1 tsp. of ground nutmeg
25g toasted almond flakes

METHOD FOR CONFIT
- Sprinkle the sea salt over the duck legs and leave to infuse for 24 hours.
- Wash the salt off the duck and pat dry with a tea towel.
- Melt the duck fat in a shallow casserole dish and add the duck legs (the fat should cover the legs). Simmer very gently for 1½ hours, turning every 20 minutes to ensure even cooking.
- Remove the duck from the fat and allow to cool, then strip the meat off the bone.

METHOD FOR PARCELS
- Combine the meat with dried cranberries and season with salt and pepper.
- Lay out spring roll wraps or cut 10cm squares of filo pastry (if using filo, it is best to use a double layer). Spoon the duck mix into the centre, fold in the sides then roll into a parcel.
- Seal the edge and paint with melted butter.
- Refrigerate until you are ready to cook them.

METHOD FOR PUREE
- Cook the broccoli in boiling salted water until soft.
- Drain and refresh with cold water.
- Place the broccoli, butter and nutmeg into blender and puree.
- Either keep the puree warm or reheat when required.

TO FINISH
- Bake the parcels in the oven for 10 minutes (180°C) until golden brown.
- Spoon broccoli puree on to each plate and arrange the parcels alongside.
- Sprinkle with toasted almonds.

PAN ROASTED QUAIL WITH PUY LENTIL, LARDON AND FRESH BEETROOT

This stylish contemporary starter, popular in my City restaurants, contrasts the wholesome flavours of puy lentils and lardon with delicate, moist quail and sweet, crisp beetroot. This is a definite 'how to impress the boss coming round to dinner' dish.

INGREDIENTS FOR 6
6 quail
250g puy lentils
1 onion, finely diced
20ml olive oil
100g lardons
2 tbsp. sherry vinegar
4 sprigs of fresh thyme, finely chopped
1 bunch of flat leaf parsley
3 fresh beetroot, ready cooked

FOR THE MARINADE
60ml sherry
60ml olive oil
1 tbsp. honey
salt and pepper
1 bay leaf
cloves
baby red chard
continental parsley to finish

METHOD
- Cut the quail into halves, bone out the rib cage leaving a breast and leg on each side. Mix together all the ingredients for the marinade, add the quail and marinate for a minimum of 2 and up to 24 hours.
- Wash the lentils thoroughly and cook in a pan of salted boiling water for 20 minutes until soft. Drain and keep to one side.
- Fry the onions in the olive oil until translucent, add the lardon and fry until crisp. Stir in the lentils, thyme and vinegar then season with salt and pepper.
- Remove the quail from marinade and fry off in a shallow pan until golden brown. Add back the marinade, cover and simmer for 5 minutes until the quail is cooked through.
- Cut the beetroot into fine julienne strips (that's a fancy term for little sticks about 30mm long and 4mm diameter).
- Arrange the red chard in a pile in the centre of individual plates and spoon warm lentils around the edge.
- Top each salad with two half quail and finish with beetroot julienne and continental parsley sprigs.

MICHAELMAS GOOSE SALAD WITH COX'S APPLES AND COBB NUTS

For me, roast goose is often a disappointment. The birds tend to produce a large amount of fat and bones, are difficult to carve at the table and yield a surprisingly little amount of meat. The flesh itself is, of course, a rich spicy delicacy and this recipe enables you to use every scrap in a delightful warm salad. A good sized duck can easily be substituted for the goose.

INGREDIENTS FOR 6–8
1 x 3kg – 4kg goose
4 cox's apples
2 tbsp. icing sugar
200g cobb nuts (gathered from Kentish hedgerows – if not, use hazelnuts like everyone else)

FOR THE DRESSING
1 tbsp. Dijon mustard
1 tbsp. dark brown sugar
3 tbsp. sherry vinegar
salt and pepper
120ml olive oil
mixed salad leaves

METHOD
- Roast the goose on a wire rack in a deep toasting tin for 1½–2 hours at 200°C (reserve the goose fat for other cooking)
- Allow the bird to cool but not chill then remove all the meat from the carcass and cut into strips.
- Core and slice the apples into wedges, paint with a little goose fat and sprinkle with icing sugar. Grill the apples until golden and soft.Keep warm.
- Roast the nuts in the oven for 10 minutes until light brown.
- Make up the dressing by combining mustard, sugar, vinegar, salt and pepper.Then add the olive oil and whisk.
- Heat the dressing in a small saucepan.
- Arrange the salad leaves on a serving platter.
- Top with strips of warm goose, apple slices and nuts.
- Spoon over the hot dressing.

MIXED GAME AND JUNIPER TERRINE

Truly rustic fare in the best tradition of City dining. This easy to make full-flavoured terrine can be adapted to whatever game you can get hold of including rabbit or hare. You will need an oblong terrine tin and a large deep roasting tin to use as a bain-marie (water bath) to bake it in.

INGREDIENTS FOR 8–10

16 rashers of bacon – streaky	zest of 2 oranges
700g mixed game – haunch of venison, pheasant, wood pigeon or duck	2 tbsp. redcurrant jelly
	100ml brandy
	4 crushed juniper berries
300g chicken liver	fresh thyme
400g sausage meat	50g pistachio nuts
1 onion, finely diced	salt and pepper
25g butter	chervil to garnish

METHOD

- Line a 1kg terrine tin with the streaky bacon, leaving the bacon long enough to fold over the top.
- Prepare and mince the game, chicken liver and sausage meat.
- Fry off the onion in butter until soft, add the orange zest, redcurrant jelly, brandy, juniper berries, fresh thyme and seasoning, cook rapidly for 2 minutes.
- Pour the mixture over the minced meats, add the pistachio nuts and stir vigorously until fully combined.
- Spoon the mixture into the lined terrine tin then fold the bacon back over the top.
- Seal the terrine with a double layer of tin foil and bake in a bain marie for 1½ hours at 200°C.
- Leave to chill over night, turn out and slice.
- Serve with Cumberland sauce (see Chapter 15) and garnish with sprigs of Chervil.

WOOD PIGEON WITH BLACK PUDDING AND DAMSON DRESSING

This is a stylish Autumnal dish with a good balance between the rich meats and fruity damsons. If you cannot get hold of damson, plums, blackberries or cherries would all do as well.

INGREDIENTS FOR 6
6 wood pigeon breasts
salt and freshly ground black
  pepper
150g black pudding
150g salad leaves
oil for frying

FOR THE DRESSING
200g damsons, halved and
  de-stoned
3 tbsp. castor sugar
30ml fino sherry vinegar
100ml sherry
1 lemon, juice only
1 tbsp. dijon mustard
salt and pepper
150ml sunflower oil

METHOD FOR DRESSING
- Cook the damsons and sugar in a saucepan gently until just starting to soften.
- Add all the ingredients for the dressing and stir it together – keep warm but do not boil to a pulp.

METHOD
- Heat some olive oil in a frying pan. Season the pigeon breasts with salt and pepper and cook them for 2–3 minutes on each side. Remove from the pan and keep warm.
- Slice the black pudding into 6 thick slices and fry for 2–3 minutes on each side.
- Divide the salad and arrange in the centre of individual plates. Top with a slice of black pudding.
- Slice each pigeon breast into 4 or 5 and place on top of the black pudding.
- Drizzle the warm dressing in a circle around the stack ensuring an even distribution of the damsons.

CHAPTER 6

DOING THE DEAL

I was chatting to a 'good City chap' the other day and he was genuinely filled with nostalgic regret for the loss of a bygone era when paperwork was something done in the morning but the real business of the City was done over lunch. A typical four-hour 'working' lunch would go something like this:

- Meet around 12.30pm for a gin and tonic in the bar and a polite session of "How's George?" "What's Miranda up to now?" "How's James getting on?" And "such a pity about Fergus."

- Lunch sharp at 1pm perhaps starting with some Potted Shrimps, Devilled Whitebait or a few Oysters washed down with a bottle or two of the Monrachet. Polite enquiries about the children leading to the much more interesting talk of old school days, "the things we got up to" and the sound thrashings that followed and "never did me any harm."

- To accompany the Château Beychevelle '75, "the Steak and Kidney Pudding looks good", maybe "the Saddle of Lamb" or even "the Grouse" now the season has begun." However, the conversation must move on to more serious things – England's chance of regaining the Ashes, golf handicaps and having moved onto a bottle of the Gevrey '82 to "try something different," a blow by blow account of how much better either of the portly gentlemen present would have performed had they been selected for last Saturday's International.

- 2.30pm triggers a half-hearted "should be getting on" but realising the subject of business is as yet untouched, the dessert menu is a better option. Jam Roly Poly, Spotted Dick, Apple Crumble, all the favourites are on offer but "what the hell should we drink with it?"

- "Always thought of Sauternes as a bit of a namby pamby ladies' drink," (premature for Champagne – no deal to celebrate at this stage).
- "Oh why not The Warres '59? Yes, bring a bottle..."

- "Port's still holding out, can't drink on an empty stomach ha ha ha – Stilton or Welsh Rarebit?" "Splendid."

- 3.30pm. "Now we muss talk about that proper... prosper... prosperition." "No need old boy, enough said, deal done." "Ah. Let's celebrate – Cliquot – the '85's outstanding."

- 4.45pm on leaving the restaurant. "Time for a pint?" "Sorry, must dash, train to catch, promised the misses I'd make it for the parents' evening." "Send the papers out in the morning. Oh, and thanks for lunch."

Those were the days – Simpsons of Cornhill, Sweetings, The Chop House or Wheelers. In stark contrast, today there is a new style of high-powered City bankers' lunch that lasts less than 45 minutes. In essence it is a very upmarket (and expensive) version of an economy class airline meal. Between 50 and 100 guests, or rather potential investors in the new financial offer, are invited at 12.45pm for 1pm. Water glasses are pre-filled; wines are opened and available on each table; some sort of sumptuous starter – for example the Foie Gras and Black Truffle Terrine with Spiced Apple and Briocheis pre-plated and laid out as aside dish. The Crème Brûleé with Piroline dessert is also pre-plated above each person's setting. Of course, these are all very busy people and no one arrives before two minutes to one. At 1pm precisely a delightful Cornish Brill with Langoustine Tails, Asparagus and Tarragon is presented irrespective of the guests having not even tried a mouthful of the Foie Gras. Immediately coffee along with ample Petit Four are placed in the centre of the tables for self-service. By 1.05pm all waiting staff are withdrawn and the presentation of the deal commences. At 1.40pm it is all over; our busy bankers rush back to their offices and computers with no requirements to even exchange pleasantries with their host; waiters clear away the majority of the 3 courses untouched: the opened but still full bottles of wine disappear behind the scenes; the client is delighted – deal done.

These may seem like extreme examples but fine food and liquor to match has always been an integral part of doing business and celebrating business done. From the infamous five investment bankers who managed to spend £44,000 on dinner at Gordon Ramsay's Petrus restaurant – so expensive were the wines they selected that dear Gordon on this occasion provided the food free of charge. Or the Hedge Fund manager who, in celebration of his day's commission earnings, put his black American Express card behind the cocktail bar at Baglioni and opened it to all comers running up a bill of £36,000. The City is a catacomb of dining rooms, bars, clubs, restaurants and venues all dedicated to providing the hospitality, cuisine and beverages required to oil the wheels of commerce and enable our great metropolis to run smoothly. Here are a few extravagant recipes with wine recommendations to match that come with a more or less foolproof guarantee of getting the deal you want. Try them at home on the boyfriend, the wife, the vicar, the landlord, even the tax collector, but not the banker – he's had it all before.

> *"...Take another glass of wine, and excuse my mentioning that society as a body does not expect one to be so strictly conscientious in emptying one's glass, as to turn it bottom upwards with the rim on one's nose." – CHARLES DICKENS*

The Bank of England and Royal Exchange

DILL BLINI WITH SMOKED SALMON, CRÈME FRAÎCHE AND KETA

Whether the smoked salmon blini are there to compliment the crisp fruity Sauvignon, or the other way around, is up to you. Either way, this is a delicious way to begin a sophisticated meal.

INGREDIENTS FOR 6

100g plain flour
1 tsp. bicarbonate of soda
1 tsp. cream of tartar
25g castor sugar
pinch of salt
1 egg
150ml milk

2 tsp. freshly chopped dill
a little oil for frying
500g smoked salmon
250ml crème fraîche
1 small jar keta caviar
1 lemon

METHOD

- Mix the flour, bicarbonate of soda, cream of tartar, sugar and salt together. In a separate bowl, mix the egg and milk then add to the dry ingredients and blend together. Add the dill.
- Heat a small amount of oil in a heavy-based frying pan. When the oil is hot, wipe it off with some kitchen paper. Using a dessert spoon drop individual rounds of the mixture into the pan. The rounds will spread a little.
- After a minute or so the bubbles will form and then burst, as they burst, flip the blini over using a palette knife and cook the other side. Remove from the pan and keep warm or reheat when needed.
- Prepare an elegant platter of sliced smoked salmon and bowls of crème fraîche, keta and wedges of lemon.
- Your guests should then help themselves to warm blini and make up their own Russian stacks.

Wine Recommendation
New Zealand Sauvignon Blanc preferably Isabel or Cloudy Bay.

BALLOTINE OF FOIE GRAS WITH HONEYCOMB AND CHARGRILLED GRAPES

The credit for this recipe must go to Karl Byron – head chef at our Just St James restaurant where he devised this incredibly simple method for preparing foie gras and came up with the unusual but sublime partner of honeycomb. We served it for the 2005 Lord Mayor's Banquet and its popularity is such that it is now permanently on the 'Just' menu.

INGREDIENTS FOR 8–10

1 kg lobe of foie gras, goose or duck liver
15g salt
10g sugar
2g finely ground white pepper
50ml Madeira

50ml brandy
1 litre chicken stock
60g honeycomb
20 seedless red grapes

METHOD FOR FOIE GRAS

- Break up the goose liver and carefully remove any skin and blood vessels.
- Season with salt, pepper and sugar then pour over the Madeira and brandy. Leave to marinade for at least 3 to 4 hours in the fridge.
- Roll the liver into a fat sausage shape 5cm in diameter. Wrap in muslin and tie each end with string. Chill overnight.
- Bring the chicken stock to the boil and then, using a thermometer, allow to cool to 75°C. Keep the chicken stock off the heat and submerge the muslin parcel in the warm stock for 30 minutes.
- Take the foie gras out of the stock and chill for 1 hour, remove from the muslin and roll in cling film to re-shape. Chill for at least 4–5 hours before serving.

TO FINISH
- Cut the grapes in half lengthways and sprinkle with a little castor sugar. Caramelise under a hot grill.
- Cut the ballotine into thin slices with a hot knife. Serve with a pile of the chargrilled grapes and a teaspoon full of honeycomb.

Wine Recommendation
Sauternes is the obvious but try a vintage Gewertztraminer or my own Nutbourne Late Harvest from West Sussex instead.

DRESSED OYSTERS WITH GINGER, LIME AND CRISPY SHALLOTS

Being an oyster lover I thought there was nothing better than freshly opened little aphrodisiacs served with lemon vinegar. That was until I tried this ginger lime dressing which took the whole experience to a new level.

INGREDIENTS FOR 36 OYSTERS
36 native oysters
crushed ice
50g pkt. crispy dried shallots

FOR GINGER LIME DRESSING
200ml sunflower oil
1 piece stem ginger shaved into small pieces
2 cloves garlic
1 lime – juice and zest
2 tbsp. light soy
1 tbsp. castor sugar
2 tsp. tobasco
freshly ground black pepper

METHOD
- To shuck the oysters, hold the shell firmly in one hand and cover the palm of the hand with a cloth to protect yourself. Slip the oyster knife between the top and bottom shells by the hinge and run the knife all the way around. This can be quite tricky, be careful not to stab yourself.
- Using a twisting motion, prise the shells apart. Try not to lose any of the liquid inside. Cut the flesh free from the shell, discard the lid and arrange the oysters on a bed of crushed ice.

METHOD FOR DRESSING
- Heat the oil in a small pan and lightly fry the ginger and garlic.
- Remove from the heat and stir in the lime juice and zest, soy, sugar, tobasco and ground black pepper.

TO FINISH
- Just before serving the oysters, spoon a tiny amount of the dressing over each and sprinkle with crispy, dried shallots.

Wine Recommendation
Californian Chardonnay, La Ina Fino Sherry or Gavi di Gavi.

St Michael's Alley

PRISM'S LANGOUSTINE AND BABY LEEK TERRINE

Prism is an elegant Harvey Nichols restaurant housed in a beautiful converted banking hall on Leadenhall Street. Their chef Jonathan Warner creates equally elegant well-executed modern British dishes such as this delicate Langoustine Terrine.

INGREDIENTS FOR 8-10

500g unsalted butter	salt and pepper
500g peeled raw medium langoustine, deveined, shells saved	6 bunches of baby leeks, trimmed
1 lemon, juiced	cayenne pepper
	1 lime, juiced

METHOD

- Slowly heat the butter over a gentle heat and when melted carefully remove the white crust from the top.
- Drain the butter into a jug leaving the milky residue behind.
- Gently reheat the clarified butter, add the langoustine shells, caramelise for 5 minutes then strain.
- Thread the langoustine on to small cocktail sticks to straighten them out. Season with salt, pepper and lemon juice. Cover with some of the melted butter and grill under a low heat for approximately 5 minutes until just cooked. Leave to cool.
- Cook the leeks in a pan of boiling salted water until just soft and then refresh in a bowl of iced water, remove the outer layer and squeeze out any excess water.
- Oil and line a small loaf tin with cling film and brush with some of the langoustine butter. Cover the base with leeks, brush with butter, season with salt, pepper and cayenne then add a layer of langoustine (sticks removed) and brush with more butter. Repeat the process to fill the tin. Cover with cling film, place weights on top and refrigerate for 24 hours.
- To serve, slice the terrine and then leave it out for 5–10 minutes to allow the butter to soften. Serve with crème fraîche and crusty bread.

Wine Recommendation
Puligny Montrachet or Meursault or if you're really going to splash out, Corton Charlemagne.

MICHAEL WINNER'S SCRAMBLED EGGS
WITH BELUGA CAVIAR

When Mr Winner told Ava Gardner how he makes scrambled eggs she said "Frank (Sinatra to you) used to do them like that." What better recommendation can you have – my own tip if you tire of the Beluga Caviar, is to grate some fresh black truffle on the eggs instead. This will still safely keep you in Michael Winner's millionaire price bracket.

INGREDIENTS FOR 4
6 eggs
200ml milk
salt and freshly ground black pepper
50g butter
100g beluga caviar (you could use a simple imitation)
4 slices buttered toast

METHOD
- Crack the eggs into a large mixing bowl, add the milk, salt and pepper then beat with an electric hand whisk until very frothy.
- Heat the butter in a non-stick frying pan until very hot. Add the egg mix and scramble with a wooden spoon.
- Before the egg fully sets, remove from the heat and stir in the caviar.
- Spoon on to hot buttered toast and serve immediately.

Wine Recommendation
Only Bollinger Grand Année, preferably 1990

CHAPTER 7

A CHINESE BANQUET

You would not normally associate the City of London with the Chinese, but there have been two memorable occasions when our Oriental friends have invaded the Guildhall.

In 1999, The People's Republic of China achieved its 50th anniversary and an instruction was sent out that every one of its embassies around the world was to host a celebratory party. China's Ambassador to Britain had recently attended the State Banquet given by the Corporation of the City to honour the Emperor of Japan. (That is another story) but the result was that I was summoned to the Chinese Embassy in Portland Place to discuss the planned celebrations.

Taking tea with the Ambassador, his entourage and various interpreters in the black and dark red, gloomy interior of the Embassy was an experience in itself. The ambitions for this great occasion were high, their approach very naïve and their budget unrealistic. It did, however, occur to me that if I said the wrong thing, I might never get out – who knew where I had been going when I disappeared? All was well and after several more visits to the Embassy, a format for the celebration was agreed. Six hundred VIP guests including politicians, judges, businessmen and all the ambassadors to Britain from around the world would attend a banquet in Guildhall. The Chinese would provide the food and the chefs; my company would provide the equipment, management and service, I would co-ordinate. The result was one of the most challenging and at the same time hilarious days of my life.

An army of chefs arrived from various Chinatown restaurants – we had agreed on thirty and around seventy turned up. To my increasing alarm, the food itself arrived in dribs and drabs throughout the day. Luckily, I was provided with two interpreters who were keen to reassure me all was normal and all would be well. The head chef was a delight and quite elderly. He spoke no English whatsoever and was clearly both pleased and amused that I would take charge of his meal.

The key to formal banqueting is planning, allocation of tasks and military style discipline. Via the interpreters we carefully set out separate divisions of chefs with individual roles and clear instructions, to be silent and concentrated throughout the meal. The signal to begin however, was like a primary school bell announcing break-time. Every single chinaman in the kitchen did his own thing; running in all directions, jabbering in different dialects, with the more senior ones attempting to shout further instructions, to no avail. Afterwards, my now 'friend for life' the head chef, smiled, bowed and nodded enthusiastically – his signal that all had gone well.

The food itself was superb, the serving of it unconventional, to put it mildly, and the result a memory never to be forgotten. There were several dishes I took note of and the Dover Sole cooked in mild chillies, star anise and coriander was to die for. It is a dish I have often served since and the recipe is detailed in the following pages.

2005 saw a very different style of Chinese banquet in the Guildhall. For the first time ever, the President of the People's Republic made a state visit to Britain and on the 2nd day of his brief stay, the Corporation of the City of London hosted a Banquet. The brief was to show off the best of British produce and cooking. The proviso was an enormous list of ingredients that the Chinese would not eat and the instruction that the visiting dignitary would insist on eating with chopsticks!

The exercise of creating a meal to meet their criteria was fascinating. All State Banquets go through a very elaborate tasting process where a chosen committee select and approve the exact meal to be served. On this occasion achieving this chopstick eating, dairy free, potato free, traditional British meal was a challenge indeed. Not to mention the Feng Shui of the angle at which certain dishes must be presented. We were, however, pleased with the result and I have shown the whole menu below. The quail breasts with a very delicate lemon and sage risotto was remarkably successful and the subtle oriental spices introduced in what was a fairly simple salad starter worked really well.

Menu served for the State Banquet for the President of China
Guildhall – 9th November 2005

Pewsey Vale, Eden Valley Riesling 2004
Prawn, Mango and Cherry Tomato Salad
With Mixed Leaves and Star Anise Dressing

* * *

Fillet of Seabass
Bok Choy and
Fresh Plum Cinnamon Glaze

* * *

Chateau Langoa Barton 1997 St Julien
Double Breast of Quail
Broad Bean and Lemon Risotto
Brochette of Bacon and Courgette

* * *

Champagne Lagache Rose NV
Passion Fruit and Blackcurrant Sorbet
With Autumn Berries
Chocolate Florentine

* * *

Baron De Sigognac VSOP Armagnac
Taylors Quinta De Vargellas 1995
Continental Blend Coffee
Petit Fours

DOVER SOLE WITH RED CHILLI, CORIANDER AND STEAMED BOK CHOY

Somehow the firm texture of dover sole, subtle oriental spices and crisp freshness of bok choy compliment one another perfectly. This very simple luxury dish is one to save for your very best friends, or just indulge yourself on your own.

INGREDIENTS FOR 6

3 x 600–750g dover sole, filleted off the bone

mild red chillies, diced very small

1 small bunch of coriander finely shredded, save some sprigs for garnish

1 tsp. ground star anise

1 tsp. salt

2 tsp. caster sugar

2 tbsp. corn flour

3 heads bok choy

light sunflower or vegetable oil for cooking

limes to garnish

METHOD

* Cut each sole fillet into three at an angle.
* In a shallow dish mix together the diced chilli, coriander, spices, salt, sugar and corn flour.
* Dip the fish into the mixture to coat both sides.
* Cook the bok choy in a large steamer over a saucepan of boiling water for 6–8 minutes.
* Drain, refresh, then cut lengthways into two and keep warm.
* Heat the oil in a shallow frying pan, then sauté the fish pieces for 3–4 minutes until golden brown and cooked through.
* Arrange the bok choy and fish on individual plates and garnish with wedges of lime and sprigs of coriander.

SIZZLE COOKED LAMB IN LETTUCE WRAPS

Wrapping is all the rage and this is certainly a 'cool' supper dish. It is best eaten as soon as it is cooked and therefore should be a kitchen table occasion. There will be a few sticky fingers around so don't bring out the best Damask.

INGREDIENTS FOR 6	FOR MARINADE
1 x 1–1.5kg boned leg of lamb	125ml sunflower oil
1 iceberg lettuce	2 tbsp. dark soy
1 cucumber	3 tbsp. dry sherry
1 bunch spring onion	1 tbsp. black bean sauce
2 red chillies, de-seeded and	2 cloves garlic, crushed
finely chopped	2 tbsp. honey
	1 tsp. chinese five spices
	1 tsp. dried chilli

METHOD
- Remove the fat from the outside of the lamb and then slice the meat as thinly as you can into small slithers.
- Combine the ingredients for the marinade, pour over the lamb and work it in. Leave for 24 hours.
- Break individual lettuce leaves into 18 small boats. Cut the cucumber and spring onion into julienne strips and arrange these items on a platter together with the lettuce and a small dish of diced chilli.
- Heat a ridged griddle pan until really hot and cook the lamb for less than one minute on each side.
- Serve immediately and invite your guests to help themselves, wrapping their own lamb in the lettuce leaves with spring onion, cucumber and chilli.

TIGER PRAWN AND MANGO SALAD

We have served this fresh tangy salad for years at parties and celebrations. It is spicy enough to be interesting whilst simple enough to appeal to almost everyone. Also try adding watermelon slices around the side of the platter to offset the chilli.

INGREDIENTS FOR 6
36 tiger prawns cooked and
  peeled
1 tsp. lime juice
salt and pepper
2 ripe mango
$\frac{1}{2}$ red pepper
1 small tin of waterchestnut,
  drained and sliced
1 bag of bean shoots
1 packet of lamb's tongue
  salad

FOR ORIENTAL DRESSING
$\frac{1}{2}$ mango (as above)
1 red chilli, de-seeded and
  finely diced
1 clove of garlic, crushed
1tbsp. thai fish sauce
2 tbsp. rice wine vinegar
3 tbsp. dark soy sauce
1 tsp. chinese 5 spices
2 tbsp. soft brown sugar
300ml sunflower oil

METHOD
- Remove the tail shells from the prawns and season with lime juice, salt and pepper. Set aside.
- Peel and stone the mango. Keep one half aside for the dressing and thinly slice the rest.
- De-seed the peppers and cut into strips.
- Arrange the beanshoots and lamb's salad on a suitable oriental platter, then scatter the mango slices, red pepper, waterchestnut and prawns on top.
- Spoon a little of the oriental dressing over and serve extra in a separate bowl.

METHOD FOR DRESSING
- Place the reserved mango and all the other ingredients except the oil in a food processor and whizz to a puree.
- Slowly pour in the oil with the motor still running to allow the ingredients to amalgamate.

THAI FISH CAKES WITH COCONUT RELISH

These delicious moreish fishcakes are quite unlike our European equivalent. Textured, a little chewy and beautifully complimented by the rich coconut relish.

INGREDIENTS FOR 18 CAKES
450g white fish (e.g. plaice or coley), skinned and cubed
1 red onion, roughly chopped
2 lime leaves
1 lemongrass stalk, chopped
1 red chilli, de-seeded and finely diced
1 small bunch coriander
1 tbsp. Thai fish sauce
1 tbsp. light soy sauce
salt
125g French beans
50g sesame seeds

COCONUT RELISH
1 egg
45g sugar
3 tbsp. Rice wine vinegar
125ml coconut milk
30g desiccated coconut
1 tbsp. light soy sauce
125ml double cream
wedges of fresh lime
sunflower oil for frying

METHOD
- Put the fish, onion, lime leaves, lemongrass, chilli, coriander, fish sauce and soy sauce into a food processor and blend until smooth. Transfer to a large mixing bowl.
- Blanch the French beans in boiling water, slice into tiny rounds and add to the mixture.
- Divide the mixture into 18 balls and then flatten into 6cm discs. Coat the cakes in sesame seeds.

METHOD FOR RELISH
- Blend the egg and sugar together in a mixing bowl. Heat the vinegar and stir it into the egg mix. Set the bowl above a pan of boiling water and cook for approximately 5 minutes, frequently stirring until very thick. Allow to cool completely.
- Stir in the coconut milk, desiccated coconut, double cream and soy.

TO FINISH

- Heat the oil in a large frying pan and fry the fishcakes for a couple of minutes on each side.
- Lift out and drain on kitchen paper. Serve with the relish on the side garnished with coriander sprigs and wedges of lime.

The Guildhall

SEARED TUNA WITH CRANBERRY INFUSION

This tangy Oriental fusion dish is hugely popular in our 'Just' restaurants. It is vital that the tuna is cooked rare and be careful not to keep boiling the infusion or it will lose its sharpness and twin colours.

INGREDIENTS FOR 6
6 x 150g tuna steaks
1½ heads of chinese leaf
salt, pepper and a little oil
1 punnet of green cress
1 orange, zested into strings
1 lemon, zested into strings

FOR THE INFUSION
1 red onion, finely diced
2 cloves garlic, thinly sliced
2 stalks lemongrass, thinly
    sliced
2 tbsp. soft brown sugar
2 tbsp. red wine vinegar
6 tbsp. dark soy sauce
150ml red wine
1 tsp. salt
300ml sunflower oil
100g frozen cranberries

METHOD
- Start by combining all the ingredients for the infusion except the cranberries in a saucepan, simmer gently for 30 minutes then add the cranberries and cook for a further 5 minutes.
- Cut the chinese leaf in quarters lengthways and blanch in boiling water. Keep warm.
- Heat a griddle pan until it is really hot. Season the tuna with salt, pepper and a little oil. Sear for 1–2 minutes on either side.
- Place a piece of chinese leaf and tuna steak on each plate, spoon the warm infusion over the fish and garnish with a mixture of cress, orange and lemon zest.

CHAPTER 8

FISH ON MONDAYS

"There is no sincerer love than the love of food."
– GEORGE BERNARD SHAW

A little known fact about the City businessman's lunchtime dining preferences (which any City based restaurateur will be able to confirm to you) is that fish is most popular on Mondays. There are several possible explanations for this.

1. A promise to the wife made after the near collapse during Sunday's lawn mowing session that the diet really will start this week – the trials and tribulations of making money then render the promise invalid from Tuesday onwards.
2. A gourmet weekend awash with rich food and fine wines resulting in a temporary lapse into healthier eating, or
3. Possibly the old adage that fish is good for the brain, and surely everyone needs a little brain food to kick start the week.

Whatever the reason, Smoked Haddock, Fillet of Sea Bass or a Plain Grilled Sole are no longer the good Catholic feasting dishes of Fridays – they're all Monday lunchtime favourites.

There is a lot to be discovered from people's menu choices in general. A good restaurant menu is an excellent barometer for the mood of the City. Rocket Salad Syndrome for example, indicates a fractious time in the markets. Business people need to prove they are lean, keen and focussed, definitely not distracted by life's small pleasures such as eating a decent lunch.

In contrast, a large Tournedos Steak is a firm indicator that things are going well – 'I deserve it, I've earned it and I can afford it' (or my over-charging wealthy host certainly can). Washed down with one of those exclusive, incredibly expensive, numbered bottled Australian Shiraz, there is a clear statement here.

Sometimes there are more subtle issues to be detected from an individual's menu selection. The rather nervous new associate dining with the "Partner" for the first time. Is he choosing the most obscure dish on the menu as his preference or in the hope of showing himself to be trendy, adventurous and ahead of the game? Or does the ambitious new sales-woman choose the same dish as her potential client in spite of her dislike for liver just so that she can say: 'Excellent choice, I will have the same.'

Finally, desserts are the best gauge of all. Sticky Toffee Pudding is well known to comfort and relieve stress. A piquant Passion Fruit Ice-cream will undoubtedly refresh and rejuvenate enthusiasm, or a generous helping of rich French Cheese will help take stock and prepare for mature decision making.

Enough of Holmes the restaurateur and back to Fish on Mondays – or any other day of the week for that matter. Here are some fabulous recipes contributed by some talented chefs from both in and out of the City.

Billingsgate Market Wharf

RICK STEIN'S CRAB FLORENTINE

Alderman David Brewer asked Rick Stein to create a recipe for his Lord Mayor's Banquet in order to promote the virtues of his Cornish home county. Rick and his team came up with this delightful little dish. All I had to do was then produce 800 of them to serve simultaneously!

INGREDIENTS FOR 6
25g unsalted butter
400g spinach, picked and washed
500g fresh picked crab meat
450ml milk
1 small onion studded with cloves
1 bay leaf
6 black peppercorns

BÉCHAMEL SAUCE
30g butter
30g flour
2 tbsp. double cream
75g parmesan, grated
1 egg yolk
1 sprig of chervil

METHOD
- Melt the unsalted butter in a heavy-bottomed pan. Add all the spinach and toss until wilted, drain in a colander and cool.
- Make a bed of spinach in 6 china dishes then top each dish with a pile of crabmeat.
- Infuse the milk with the onion, bay leaf and peppercorns.
- Melt the butter in a pan. Add the flour and cook for 1 minute, then whisk in the infused milk to form a sauce.
- Stir in the cream and parmesan then cook for a further 5 minutes on a low heat.
- Remove from the heat, whisk in the egg yolk and check the seasoning.
- Spoon the sauce over the crab and spinach and grill for 5 minutes until golden brown.
- Garnish with chervil and serve immediately.

ANTON MOSSIMAN'S MARINATED SALMON WITH CRABMEAT AND LEMON DRESSING

Anton's reputation both in and out of the City for clean striking flavours is second to none. He is a master chef in the proper old-fashioned sense of the word and a good friend.

INGREDIENTS FOR 6
500g salmon fillet with
   skin on
120g crabmeat
1 small bunch chives, chopped
12 sprigs coriander, chopped
3 spring onions, sliced
20g pickled ginger, sliced

MARINADE FOR SALMON
100g sea salt
100g castor sugar
20g white pepper
20g star anise
20g coriander seeds
2 sticks lemongrass

FOR DRESSING
juice of 4 lemons
50g sugar
1 teaspoon arrowroot
20ml light soy

200ml olive oil
zest of 2 lemons
100ml brandy

METHOD
- Blend all the marinade ingredients together in a food processor. Spread the mixture over the whole length of salmon. Chill and marinate for 24 hours.
- Scrape off the marinade and remove the skin. Slice the salmon in ¼cm thin slices.
- To make the dressing bring the lemon juice and sugar to the boil, mix the arrowroot with the soy then add to the boiling lemon to make a thick sauce. Remove from the heat and whisk in the olive oil.
- Using a 5 inch ring or pastry cutter to contain the ingredients on 6 individual plates, layer first the salmon and then the crab meat, and finally top with chives, coriander, spring onion and ginger. Remove the ring.
- To finish, drizzle over the lemon dressing.

FILLET OF SOLE, MINTED PEA PUREE AND BALSAMIC REDUCTION

A favourite at my original City restaurant, Just Gladwins – healthy, simple components, lovely fresh colours and a hint of glamour with the addition of the spirals of balsamic.

INGREDIENTS FOR 6

6 x 170g lemon sole fillets
340g of frozen peas handful of fresh mint,
6 sprigs for garnish
30g butter
125ml double cream

salt and pepper
rind of a lemon, cut into strings
balsamic reduction (see chapter 15)

METHOD

- Trim the sole fillets and fold in half – season with salt and pepper.Place in a buttered tin and cover with buttered greaseproof paper ready to cook.
- Cook the peas in a pan of boiling salted water until soft.
- Whilst the peas are cooking, select 6 nice mint leaf heads for garnish, then pull the remaining leaves off the stalks and roughly chop.Once the peas are cooked, drain them thoroughly and puree in a food processor with the mint, butter and double cream. Check seasoning to taste. Keep warm.
- Preheat the oven to 200°C. Bake the Sole for 8–10 minutes until cooked but still pearly. Serve on a bed of the pea puree and finish with lemon strings, a mint sprig and a drizzle of balsamic reduction.

MEDALLIONS OF MONKFISH WITH ASPARAGUS, CROUTONS & MUSTARD SEED DRESSING

This is a delicious warm fish salad suitable as a main course or starter. Monkfish being a meaty, robust fish, takes the citrus and mustard flavours well. It is also an excellent dish with the fish cooked on the barbecue.

INGREDIENTS FOR 6
750g monkfish tail
18 sticks of asparagus
2 slices of white bread cut
  into small cubes
115g butter
1 tbsp. olive oil
1 bag mixed salad leaves

FOR THE MUSTARD SEED DRESSING
1 lemon, rind and juice
1 orange, rind and juice
100ml white wine
1 tbsp. dijon mustard
2 tbsp. grainy mustard
1 tbsp. lemon vinegar
1 tbsp. castor sugar
salt, pepper and tabasco
300ml olive oil

METHOD
- Whisk all the ingredients for the dressing together and heat gently in a saucepan.
- Trim the asparagus and cook for about 7 minutes in boiling water. Drain and refresh in cold water.
- Cut the monkfish tails into 12 disks and season with salt, pepper and oil.
- In a frying pan melt the butter with the olive oil and cook the bread, turning constantly until golden in colour.
- Heat a ridged griddle pan until really hot and cook the monkfish, 2–3 minutes on each side.
- Arrange the salad on a platter and scatter on the asparagus.
- Place the fish medallions on top. Spoon over the warm dressing and sprinkle with croutons. Serve immediately.

THE MANSION HOUSE SEARED DEVON SCALLOPS
WITH WHITE BEAN BROTH

Rather than the name of a tube station where perhaps you can purchase a Mars bar to eat, Mansion House is the palatial residence of The Lord Mayor of London. Searcy's, led by their development chef Giles Thompson, spoil the Mayoralty and guests by the preparation of such delicacies as this dish of Devon Scallops in a frothy bean broth.

INGREDIENTS FOR BROTH FOR 6
100g coco beans
2 tbsp. olive oil
50g onion, chopped
25g smoked bacon
100ml chicken stock
100ml double cream
10ml truffle oil
30g butter chervil to garnish
salt and pepper

FOR THE SCALLOPS
12 x king scallops
80g broad beans, cooked and peeled
40g borlotti beans, fresh or tinned
40g flageolet beans, fresh or tinned
40g celeriac
20g black truffle, cut into julienne strips

METHOD FOR BROTH
- Soak the coco beans overnight.
- In a heavy-based saucepan, heat the olive oil and gently cook the onions and bacon. Add the coco beans and cover with the chicken stock, season and bring to the boil. Cook for approximately 1½ hours until tender.
- Remove the bacon and blend the beans in a liquidiser, adding more stock if necessary.
- Reheat the bean puree in a saucepan with the cream, truffle oil and butter. Froth with a hand blender. Season with salt and pepper.

METHOD FOR SCALLOPS
- Cook the broad, borlotti and flageolet beans in salted boiling water until tender.
- Cut the celeriac into julienne strips and deep-fry until crisp. Set aside.

- In a hot non-stick pan sear the scallops with a little olive oil for 2–3 minutes until both sides are caramelised.
- Drain the beans, spoon into the bottom of soup bowls then place the seared scallops in the centre and pour around the frothy broth.
- Garnish with the crispy celeriac and truffle julienne.

CHAPTER 9

CRIME AND PUNISHMENT

Every great city has its share of intrigue, crime, corruption and punishment and The City of London, with nearly two millenniums of history, is certainly no exception.

The Old Bailey 17th April 1779:

> *Mary Owen... was indicted for the wilful murder of Henry Owen... or*
> *that she feloniously, traitorously, and wilfully, and of her malice aore -*
> *hought did mix and mingle a large quantity of deadly poison called*
> *arsenick, into a cake made of dough, which cake she caused and*
> *procured to be baked, and did give the said Henry the said cake to*
> *eat... ,*

The full recipe for the cake is not recorded but I suspect there would have been raisins, dates, almonds and other tasty ingredients mixed in with the arsenic and dough to tempt the said Henry to eat it.

In the 18th and 19th Century the Central Criminal Courts at Old Bailey had a certain preoccupation with eating and drinking – not only did many of the crimes involve stealing, over imbibing, violence under the influence or even murder by food or beverage, but the judges themselves were often found the worst for lunch. Dining was a key part of the court sessions and it was customary for the City Sheriff and Aldermen to host two dinners each day in order that judges and court officials might attend either sitting. It was not uncommon, however, for the more indulgent to attend both and whilst the first course would vary, the second was always large quantities of beef steaks. Wine also flowed freely. There is a record dated 1807 stating that 145 dozen bottles of wine were consumed over 19 days of court sessions. Often the judges would pass sentence having been disturbed from their feasting with "their wigs well oiled". A death sentence was quickly issued and then the real business of City dining could recommence.

Luncheon at the Old Bailey today has a much more regulated format –The City Sheriffs still entertain the judges but to an extraordinarily strict timetable:

12.30pm	Sheriff's guests arrive.
1.00pm	Judges assemble.
1.10pm	Gong sounds and the Duty Alderman accompanies the Senior Judge present into the dining room.
1.55pm	Doors open, lunch ends.

The only exception is for Royal visits when the judges assemble at 12.30 rather than 1pm. Lunch, however, still concludes at 1.55pm – no time for debauchery anymore. Going back in time once again, the unfortunate criminals did not fare quite so well as their judges. The following is a summary of the 1817 dietary plan for Newgate Jail:

Breakfast:	8oz bread and 1 pint gruel seasoned on alternate days with molasses and salt.
Dinner:	on alternate days: 8oz bread, 3oz cooked meat, 8oz potato or 8oz bread, 1 pt soup containing 3oz meat and vegetables.
Supper:	The same as breakfast.
Female Prisoners:	As above but 6oz instead of 8oz of bread each meal.

Very well regulated but not a restaurant to queue up for. Not all prison accommodation in the City was quite so frugal. Among many other famous and noble prisoners charged with high treason and held in the Tower of London was King John the Good of France. Held prisoner in 1360 he had with him an entire entourage of a tailor, a secretary, a maitre d'hotel, a jester, various other attendants and even an organist. In one day he was supplied with 12 chickens, a whole veal calf, 3 carcasses of mutton, 74 loaves of bread, 12 pounds of almonds, 8 sesters (whatever they may have been) and 21 gallons of wine. The prisoner even invited King Edward and Queen Philippa to a banquet at the Tower during his captivity.

In charge of the City's Fortress is the Constable of the Tower. It is possibly the oldest office in the UK dating from 1078 when William the Conqueror built the Tower and installed his first Constable. It was a position of great prestige and wealth; even today it includes a promise from the Monarch that every ship or gallery coming to the

City with wine will give the Constable a contribution from their cargo. The instructions, restated every 5 years when a new Constable is installed are very specific, making sure that one gallon comes from the hold behind the mast and one from the fore, presumably to ensure the captain does not hold back the good stuff. I am not sure whether any wine still enters this country via the Thames but sadly, although the ruling still stands, it is apparently no longer practised. Who wants to be a Constable these days?

Crime in the City today rarely involves food, wine or even high treason. Instead it centres around money. Insider share dealings, multibillion pound bond frauds, stealing pension funds or bringing down banks. Half of the infamous businessmen involved in these crimes have been my customers before their downfall. And why do they do it? To host more lavish parties? To eat caviar on their yachts? Or to drink Cristal Champagne in their nightclubs? Whichever it is they are missing out. Even if dinner in their own prisons is brought in from The Fat Duck or the wine list is from the Gavroche there is no substitute for making your own Fishcakes, Crab Chowder or Smoked Haddock Pie – these are the good things in life, who needs crime or punishment?

"Claret is the liquor for boys; port for men; but he who aspires to be a hero must drink brandy. In the first place, brandy is most grateful to the palate; and then brandy will do soonest for a man what drinking can do for him. Thee are, indeed, few who are able to drink brandy. That is a power rather to be wished for than attained."
– SAMUEL JOHNSON

COD AND ROCKET FISHCAKES WITH SEASONED CRÈME FRAÎCHE

Why is it that fishcakes on a menu in any City restaurant is an instant hit? They fall into that comfort food zone – tasty, easy to eat and probably Nanny used to make them!

INGREDIENTS FOR 12 CAKES

600g cod	salt and pepper
1 bay leaf	flour for coating
a few peppercorns	2 eggs mixed with a little salt
400g peeled potatoes, maris piper	150g fresh white breadcrumbs
100g fresh rocket	oil for frying
1 tbsp. anchovy essence	300ml crème fraîche
1 tbsp. lemon juice	salt and pepper
	1 lemon cut into wedges

METHOD

- Place the cod, bay leaf and peppercorns in a deep roasting tin, cover with water then poach on the hob for 10–15 minutes. Remove the fish from the liquid and set aside.
- Cook the potatoes in boiling salted water for 20–25 minutes until tender and then mash.
- Roughly chop the rocket, flake the cod and combine with the mashed potato, anchovy essence and lemon juice. Season with salt and pepper.
- Shape the mixture into 12 balls and then flatten (not too perfect – we want them to look homemade).
- Coat the fishcakes in seasoned flour then in the egg mixture and finally in the breadcrumbs, making sure that they are fully covered.
- Heat oil in a shallow frying pan and cook the fishcakes on each side for 4–5 minutes until golden brown.
- Serve the fishcakes with seasoned crème fraîche and wedges of lemon to garnish.

TWICE BAKED CELERIAC AND SALMON SOUFFLÉ

This is a highly versatile dish that can be adapted to most things in your fridge. Almost any cheese can be substituted for the cheddar, and the celeriac and salmon can be swapped for spinach, broccoli, bacon, ham, prawns – you name it. The secret of these foolproof soufflés is that they are first baked in a bain-marie then re-baked dry when ready to serve.

INGREDIENTS FOR 6

30g butter	150g cooked salmon – flaked
30g self raising flour	a few chopped chives
250ml milk	salt and pepper
60g grated cheddar cheese	2 eggs, separated
75g cooked and grated celeriac	a little fresh grated parmesan

METHOD

- Butter 6 ramekin dishes.
- In a heavy-bottomed saucepan melt the butter, then stir in the self raising flour and cook for 1 minute.
- Add the milk to the saucepan and bring back to the boil, stirring all the time to avoid lumps.
- Stir in the cheese, celeriac , salmon, chives and season with salt and pepper.
- Take the pan off the heat, stir in the egg yolks and transfer to a large mixing bowl.
- Whisk the egg white to soft peaks and fold into the celeriac mixture.
- Spoon into the ramekins and sprinkle with parmesan.
- Place the ramekins in a roasting tin half filled with water to make a bain-marie.
- Bake at 180°C for 20–25 minutes until golden. Remove from the oven and leave to get cold – they will sink a little.
- When you want to serve the soufflés, take them out of the ramekins and place on a tin lined with baking paper, re-bake at 200°C for 10–15 minutes until puffed up and perfect.
- Serve with a little dressed salad and a salsa (see chapter 15).

CLAM CHOWDER

This particular gruel – rather more attractively called a chowder, is certainly no punishment to eat, but it does meet the criteria of Newgate Prison by being a complete meal in one dish. Perhaps you should try presenting it to your husband, wife or partner on this basis and see what they say.

INGREDIENTS FOR 6–8

24 large clams
40g butter
75g bacon, thinly sliced
1 onion, finely diced
350g potatoes, peeled and
    diced
450ml milk
180ml double cream

1 bay leaf
150g white fish, skinned and
    cut into pieces
2 plum tomatoes, de-seeded
    and diced
salt and pepper
small bunch parsley

METHOD

- Wash and scrub the clams and place in a large pan with 100ml of water. Cover with a lid and cook over a high heat until the clams open.
- Remove from the heat and drain in a colander, reserving the cooking liquid. Remove the meat from half the clams and cut in half. Leave the rest in the shells.
- Melt the butter in a pan, fry the bacon until it starts to brown, add the onions and cook until soft.
- Put the potatoes, milk, cream and bay leaf in a large saucepan. Bring to the boil and then reduce to a simmer until the potatoes are cooked but still firm.
- Add the onion, bacon and reserved cooking liquor from the clams. Simmer for a further 5 minutes, add the fish and continue to simmer until cooked through. Add the clam meat and tomato and season with salt and freshly ground black pepper
- Serve garnished with chopped parsley and the remaining clams in shells.

FILLET OF SEABASS WITH LEMON RISOTTO

Seabass has come of age. 10 years ago it was still an expensive, speciality fish you might encounter in Michelin star restaurants. Now farmed fairly healthily in large sea based enclosures throughout the Mediterranean it is readily available in every bistro, brasserie or gastro pub. Best filleted and served with the skin on, these tender fish need simple cooking and minimum fussing over.

INGREDIENTS FOR 6
6 x 150g seabass fillets,
  skin on
a little olive oil
salt and pepper
2 small lemons

FOR THE RISOTTO
4 tbsp. olive oil
1 medium white onion, diced
350g arborio rice
salt
1 litre vegetable stock
3 lemons, rind and juice
150ml double cream
150g freshly grated parmesan
  cheese
1 pkt. chives, chopped

METHOD FOR RISOTTO
- Heat the olive oil a large heavy-based saucepan and cook the diced onion for about 5 minutes until it begins to soften.
- Now stir in the rice and heat through for a minute until shiny and opaque.
- Turn down the heat and add the stock and lemon juice a ladle at a time – allow the rice to absorb the liquid before adding any more – this should take 20–25 minutes, stirring regularly.
- When the rice feels soft and fluffy and the texture is creamy but firm the risotto is ready. Stir in the lemon rind, double cream, grated parmesan and chives.

METHOD FOR FISH
- Season the seabass with olive oil, salt and freshly ground black pepper. Preheat a ridged griddle pan and cook the fillets skin side down for 3–4 minutes until the skin is golden and crispy. Turn over and briefly cook the other side.

- Cut the ends of the lemons and slice each of them into 3 disks. Sear them on the griddle alongside the fish until caramelised.
- Present the seabass skin up with the lemons on top and serve the risotto alongside.

Dining Room at Old Bailey

SIR MENZIES' SMOKED HADDOCK PIE

A perfect politician's recipe: Sir Menzies Campbell's Smoked Haddock Pie is recommended on the grounds that it will keep warm indefinitely in a low oven – is this for the late hour he may eventually get to eat it or the moment his party is finally recognised? Either way, it is a delightful simple recipe and one of my favourites too.

INGREDIENTS FOR 6
450g smoked haddock fillets
600ml milk
225g fresh leaf spinach,
  washed
6 tomatoes, sliced
6 hard boiled eggs, sliced
salt and pepper

FOR CHEESE SAUCE
50g butter
25g flour
100g grated cheese

METHOD
• Place the haddock in a deep roasting dish. Pour over the milk and cook over a medium heat for 15 minutes.
• Remove the fish, allow it to cool a little then flake the flesh into pieces discarding any bones. Strain the cooking liquid and set aside for the cheese sauce.
• Cover the base of an ovenproof dish with the spinach, followed by a layer of flaked haddock, then the hard-boiled eggs and finally the sliced tomatoes. Season with salt and pepper between each layer.

METHOD FOR CHEESE SAUCE
• Melt the butter in a saucepan over a medium heat. Add the flour and allow to cook for a minute or two.
• Gradually add the reserved cooking liquid a little at a time, whisking continuously to get a smooth sauce. Once all the milk has been added and the sauce has thickened, stir in the cheese and allow it to melt.
• Spoon the cheese sauce over the haddock dish and cook in the oven at 180°C for 20–30 minutes.

CHAPTER 10

GOOD ENOUGH FOR ROYALTY

My own day began at 4.30 in the morning in a field of blackcurrants near my West Sussex home. We were selecting and picking 1000 blackcurrant leaves, each precisely 2½ inch diameter – the perfect garnish for chilled soufflé of early summer berries. It was the day the world would be commemorating 50 years since VE Day officially ended the Second World War and Her Majesty the Queen was the principle host at a banquet to surpass all others in the City of London.

I had cooked for The Queen and The Duke of Edinburgh on quite a few occasions before, sometimes at intimate private dinner parties where they were clearly off duty .At one such soiree I was introduced to Her Majesty and to my great embarrassment and Prince Philip's great amusement managed to call her Your Royal Highness – a title she had moved on from at the Coronation in 1952. The Prince very audibly whispered in her ear "the chef thinks you look very young, Elizabeth."

However, despite any previous faux pas, on 6th May 1995 the City had somehow chosen me and my team to cater for this momentous VE Day celebration. 52 Heads of State from around the world were present, another 180 countries were represented by their vice presidents, ministers or ambassadors. The Guildhall's Great Hall was filled to its capacity of 720 guests but to accommodate everyone, two additional areas were simultaneously served the same banquet, giving a total of 1004 diners. Our own staff, supplemented from every possible catering outlet, friends of friends and volunteers numbered 280. Add to this the trumpeters, the pikemen, the military bands, the security and the hangers on – and like me, you have lost count. There were requirements for organisers' lunches, police refreshments, committee members' teas and VIP receptions in addition to the banquet itself. All together, the guest list, splendour and opulence of the occasion was a Royal Banquet without equal. Here is the menu:

Banquet in the presence of HM Queen Elizabeth II to commemorate the 50th Anniversary of V.E. day May 1995

Stoneliegh Chardonnay 1993
Lobster of the Western Approaches
With a Julienne of English Asparagus and Nasturtium Flowers

***

Escalope of Poached Atlantic Turbot
tied with Ribbons of Scottish Smoked Salmon
Welsh Leeks served with a Watercress Sauce

***

Garden of England Sorbet

***

Château Prieure Lichine 1982
Roast Beef of Old England
Yorkshire Puddings
Jersey Royals
Carrot and Swede Puree
Brown Brothers Orange Flora Muscat 1994

***

Chilled Soufflé of Early Summer Berries
Warres 1970 Delamaine 1963

Coffee
Petit Fours

The City does, of course, have a great history of Royal connections. Its wealth and immense power in the 16th and 17th Centuries was only tolerated because of the huge financial support the Corporation and livery companies gave to the monarchy. The Lord Mayor and Aldermen were a seat of government to rival Parliament and their opulent feasting was second to none. Today there is a long established tradition of the City hosting major Royal occasions.

The Queen and Duke of Edinburgh's golden wedding anniversary was celebrated with a luncheon in Guildhall in November 1997 and then in June 2000 when the whole country was celebrating the Queen Mother's one hundredth birthday, another commemorative state occasion was hosted by The Lord Mayor and Corporation. This was a wholly non-political affair, beautifully focussed on simply pleasing the birthday girl. Brocade tablecloths, flowers, wines and menu were all chosen to suit. Luncheon comprised of Scottish lobster, Welsh saddle of lamb and Eton mess – apparently Her Majesty's favourite, an irresistible concoction of mashed strawberry, meringue, cream and kirsch. The menus themselves were printed on silk scrolls as a commemorative trophy for each guest to take home.

It was an occasion pitched just right. Only enhanced by the incident in the midst of her speech when the Queen Mum accused the Archbishop of Canterbury of stealing her glass of wine – a hilarious moment shared by the company, the press and the nation as a whole.

Following the success of these and many other great City banquets, the Corporation was again called upon to host a celebration of the Queen's Golden Jubilee and I was again fortunate to be involved. A church service at St Paul's, luncheon at Guildhall, procession along The Mall, rock concert in Buckingham Palace gardens and a fly past of Concord all combined to be a fitting mix to commemorate 50 years of our Monarch's reign. The City's luncheon sort to encompass guests from all over Britain and every walk of life. Selected school children were seated next to members of the Royal family and charity workers were in conversation with our political leaders. It was another momentous catering day for our team and made extra special by an invitation for the entire catering staff – chefs, managers, porters, waiting staff, washer uppers et al to line

Guildhall yard to cheer off Her Majesty's departure. A sight straight out of Bride's Head Revisited – while the Queen gaveus her gentle wave, Prince Philip mimed his own applause back to us acknowledging our efforts. Here is the menu served on that wonderful Jubilee day and following it are a selection of main course recipes which have a track record proving them to be fit for Royalty.

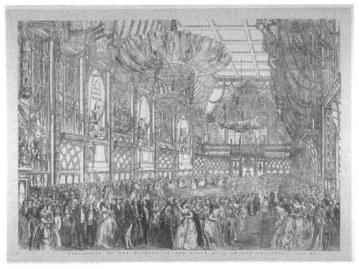

Procession of Queen Victoria to the State Ball in the Guildhall

Bouquet of Asparagus With Scottish Smoked Salmon

Sancerre, Domaine de la Moussiére, Mellot 2000.

***

Tournedos of Beef
Crowned with a Golden Soufflé of Globe Artichoke
Sage Butter Sauce
Jersey Royal New Potatoes
Fine Green Beans

***

Chateau Léoville Barton 1989

Meringue Vacherin, Pearls of Passion Fruit, Raspberry
and Spiced Orange Ice Cream

Family Reserve Noble Riesling, Kings Valley, 1997

Coffee
Petit Fours

Dalwhinnie 15 years old

DUKE OF KENT'S BEEF STEW

It was an honour in itself to receive such elegant and polite refusals from most members of the Royal family wishing this book every success, but regretfully saying it would not be appropriate for them to contribute. Not so the Duke of Kent – and what a fine, robust English recipe it is too – many thanks Your Royal Highness.

INGREDIENTS 6–8

500g braising steak, cubed	1 dstsp. flour
2 tsp. olive oil	275ml red wine
6 shallots, peeled	1 small tin of tomatoes
1 clove garlic, finely chopped	110g flat mushrooms, thickly
1 tbsp. thyme leaves chopped	sliced
1 bay leaf	1 red pepper, de-seeded and
salt and pepper	cut into strips

METHOD

- Preheat the oven to 140°C.
- In a flame-proof casserole dish heat 1 tsp. of olive oil until very hot, then brown the beef on all sides. Remove and set aside. Add the rest of the oil and then brown the shallots and garlic.
- Return the meat and juices to the pan, add the thyme, bay leaf, salt and pepper then stir in the flour and let it absorb the juices.
- Add the red wine a little at a time, stirring well, then the tomatoes and mushrooms and stir. Bring to a simmer, cover with a lid and place in the oven for 1½ hours.
- Add the red pepper and return to the oven for a further 30–40 minutes until the pepper is cooked.

TOURNEDOS OF BEEF CROWNED WITH A GOLDEN ARTICHOKE SOUFFLÉ

This memorable dish I originally created for The Queen's Golden Jubilee Banquet is both impressive and delicious. Understandably it has been served on many 'golden' occasions and anniversaries since but none quite as eminent as the original. Give yourself time as there are several stages to follow.

INGREDIENTS FOR 6
6 x 170g Tournedos steaks
6 x globe artichoke fonds
watercress and fresh redcurrants to decorate

INGREDIENTS FOR THE SOUFFLÉ
20g butter
20g self-raising flour
150ml milk
100g cheddar cheese, grated
2 eggs, separated
100g artichoke hearts, chopped
¼ bunch chives, chopped
20g butter for ramekins
20g grated parmesan

INGREDIENTS FOR THE SAGE BUTTER
115g butter
1 tbsp. sherry vinegar
2 tsp. dijon mustard
1 tbsp. soft dark brown sugar
50ml white wine
8 sage leaves finely shredded
salt and freshly ground black pepper

METHOD FOR SOUFFLÉS
• Please see the Celeriac and Salmon Soufflé in the previous chapter and follow the method exactly substituting the chopped artichokes for the celeriac and fish.

METHOD FOR SAGE BUTTER
• Place all the ingredients in a small pan and heat gently until the butter has melted.
• Simmer for 10 minutes then check the seasoning.

METHOD FOR STEAKS
• Seal the steaks on all sides in a hot griddle pan then transfer to a small ovenproof dish.

- Neatly fit the turned out twice-baked soufflés into the artichoke fonds and secure them on to the top of each steak with a cocktail stick.
- Bake in a preheated oven at 200°C for 7–10 minutes.
- Serve the steaks with the sage butter, a sprig of watercress and a small sprig of redcurrants on top of the crown.

"People who have tried it, tell me that a clear conscience makes you very happy and contented; but a full stomach does the business quite as well, and is cheaper, and more easily obtained."
– JEROME K. JEROME

BREAST OF DUCK WITH RASPBERRIES, RED ONION AND TARRAGON

Served on the occasion of the Queen and Duke of Edinburgh's Golden Wedding Anniversary, this is a lovely celebratory dish full of colour and exciting flavours. The Asparagus and Bean Bundles detailed in the chapter 'Going to Market' will be perfect to go with it.

INGREDIENTS FOR 6
6 x 200g duck breasts
2 red onions, thinly sliced
15g butter
1 tbsp. raspberry vinegar
1 tbsp. castor sugar
salt and pepper
1 punnet of raspberries
tarragon to garnish

FOR THE TARRAGON JUS
400ml duck or chicken stock
200ml red wine
2 tbsp. raspberry vinegar
1 tbsp. lemon juice
1 tbsp. dijon mustard
2 stalks of fresh tarragon
1 tbsp. soft brown sugar
salt and pepper
2 tsp. arrowroot

METHOD FOR TARRAGON JUS
- Place all the ingredients except the arrowroot in a saucepan and bring to the boil. Turn the heat down and simmer gently for 30–40 minutes.
- Just before serving, remove the tarragon, mix the arrowroot with a little cold water, bring the sauce back to the boil, add the arrowroot and allow to thicken.

METHOD FOR RASPBERRIES AND RED ONION
- Heat the butter gently in a heavy-based frying pan and cook the onions until they are soft. Add the raspberry vinegar, sugar, salt and pepper and cook until the liquid has evaporated. Stir in the fresh raspberries and keep warm.

METHOD FOR DUCK

- Heat a little oil in a heavy-based pan. Season the duck breast with salt and pepper and cook skin side down for about 10 minutes so that the fat dissolves and the skin is a nice dark brown colour. Turn over and seal briefly on the other side.
- Transfer the breasts to a roasting tin and roast in the oven at 200°C for 10 minutes.
- Allow the duck to rest for 5–10 minutes then slice each breast arranging a crescent of slices on each plate. Garnish with the raspberry and red onion mixture, spoon over the tarragon jus and sprinkle chopped tarragon on top.

LOBSTER THERMIDOR

What better company could you keep – The Queen Mother's hundredth birthday party in Guildhall – when the Archbishop may have got her wine but no one was going to deny Her Majesty the Lobster Thermidor.This is a timeless classic recipe which I am sure will still be with us in another 100 years time.

INGREDIENTS FOR 6

3 x 750g–1kg lobsters, cooked
½ tbsp. lemon vinegar
salt, pepper and tabasco
20g grated parmesan
45g butter
1 shallot, finely chopped
45g flour

285ml fresh fish stock
55ml white wine
100ml double cream
½ tsp. english mustard
2 tbsp. parsley, chopped
½ lemon juice only

METHOD

- Cut the lobsters in half using a heavy knife inserted into the cross behind the lobster's head. Cut down between the eyes all the way through and then turn around and cut down along the tail.
- Remove the meat from the tail and head and set aside. Crack the claws and extract the meat. Wash the shells and leave to drain.
- Roughly chop all the lobster meat – season with salt, pepper, lemon vinegar and Tabasco and then put the meat back in the shells.
- For the sauce, melt the butter in a pan and cook the shallot until it has softened. Stir in the flour and cook for 2 minutes.
- Stir in the stock, wine and double cream and bring to the boil. Add the mustard, herbs, lemon juice and seasoning.
- Carefully spoon the sauce over the half lobster, sprinkle with the parmesan and cook under a preheated grill for 3–4 minutes until golden brown.

ANTONY WORRALL THOMPSON'S CROWN ROAST OF LAMB

Antony Worrall Thompson is one of this country's great foodies. An entrepreneur, a restaurateur, TV celebrity chef but most of all, an expounder of fine cooking. This classic crown of lamb is a traditional British roast at its very best.

INGREDIENTS FOR 6
1 x 16 cutlet crown roast of lamb (ask your butcher to prepare)
3 cloves of garlic, chopped
1 tsp. thyme leaves
1 tsp. rosemary leaves
1 tsp. maldon salt
½ tsp. ground black pepper

FOR THE SAUCE
600ml lamb stock and lamb juices
1 tbsp. corn flour
150ml double cream
3 tbsp. ruby port
watercress to garnish

METHOD
- Mix the garlic, thyme, rosemary, salt and pepper together to make a smooth paste and spread it over the lamb.
- Fill the centre of the crown with a ball of foil to keep the shape and cover the end of each bone with foil to prevent burning.
- Place the lamb in roasting tin, add a third of the lamb stock, 3 tbsp. water and roast in a preheated oven at 220°C for 20 minutes. Reduce to 180°C and cook for a further 15 minutes.
- Remove the lamb from the oven and allow it to rest for 10 minutes before serving.
- Add the remainder of the stock to the roasting tin and bring it to the boil. Then strain into a saucepan and return it to the heat.
- Mix the corn flour, cream and port together and pour it slowly into the lamb stock, whisking constantly. Stir until thickened then season to taste.
- Remove the foil from the lamb and fill the centre with watercress. Present the whole crown to the table then carve. Serve sauce separately.

CHAPTER 11

CITY SKIES

Surely a city that can boast a vast statue of a gherkin is a place dedicated to eating. If the architect and planners had got together properly we could be sprouting an entire market garden of new City buildings. Imagine a globe artichoke above Liverpool Street Station, a bulging butternut squash complete with matching yellow interior on Queen Victoria Street and an enormous raspberry next to St Paul's – no more high finance in the City of London, just street markets, cafés, restaurants and food stores.

In fact, the Swiss RE Tower is rather modestly named number 30 St Mary Axe and when I went to visit, there was not a pickled vegetable in sight. It stands a magnificent 180 metres high with the equivalent of 5 football pitches of glass cladding stuck to the sides. There is apparently a beautiful restaurant and several dining rooms on the 38th floor but alas, all reserved exclusively for the use of the building's occupants and their guests. Even the menus and recipes are exclusive. I made repeated pleas for a recipe contribution from the inspired and somewhat volatile chef, Richard Corrigan, but to no avail. Perhaps he was afraid of some old jokes sneaking in, such as a speciality Pickled Cucumber Soup, a Warm Cornichon Salad or just plain Wallys and Cheese on Toast.

Sky dining is available elsewhere in the City. Tower 42 (again renamed from a previous life as The Nat West Tower after the bank was swallowed up) on its top floor offers 'Vertigo'– a champagne bar, eatery and giddy illness all in one. Lower down the tower on floor 24 there is also a fine dining restaurant operated by the Roux Brothers brand. Although not nearly so many floors up, Terence Conran's rooftop restaurant 'Coq D'Argent', wittily named after its location in Poultry, is the City's most chic sky-high restaurant and so it should be, having been created by one of the country's finest designers.

In the late 1980s and early 1990s when new high rise office blocks were appearing on the City skyline every week, I had the opportunity to cook in most of them prior to being let. Property agents and surveyors came to some mutual understanding that they would take it in turns to each persuade their instructing developers to host lavish parties for themselves and their colleagues in order to successfully launch their new buildings on to the market. This entertaining frenzy really took off and we were supplying temporary kitchens, furnishings and fabulous hospitality in a different new office block 2 or 3 times a week.

Unfortunately, one open plan floor looks pretty much the same as the next and with the same guest list, a constant supply of novelty themes had to be incorporated to keep the rage going. Ranging from ice sculptures and casino tables, to hospitality girls, school dinners or indoor fairgrounds – new agents on the block did not know what had hit them and the only answer was to reciprocate by persuading their own property owners – "the only way to get interest in this white elephant is to serve more lobster and champagne than anyone else." Thankfully, as the City came out of recession, the new buildings began to sell, surveyors began to have work to do and learnt to buy their own lunch.

Lavish launches for flagship new buildings still take place in the City but in a somewhat more selective way and talking of selective hospitality, here are a set of delightful elegant main course dishes together with recommendations for wines ready to lift you to the sky.

ANTON MOSSIMAN'S POACHED CHICKEN BREAST WITH BABY LEEKS AND TROMPETTE MUSHROOMS AND A TOMATO HERB DRESSING

Almost the perfect healthy diet – minimum fat and a modern cooking method which retains all natural goodness and flavour in the food. Cling film is a most versatile cooking tool – you will be amazed how well it survives in the boiling stock – just don't try roasting it in the oven!

INGREDIENTS FOR 6
6 medium sized chicken breasts
salt and pepper
12 baby leeks, blanched in salted water
100g trompette mushrooms, cut into halves
2 pints chicken stock

FOR TOMATO DRESSING
50ml sherry vinegar
1 shallot, finely diced
3 plum tomatoes, blanched, de-seeded and finely chopped
mixed fresh herbs e.g. chives, chervil, and basil, chopped

METHOD
- Remove the skin from the chicken breast. 'Butterfly' the chicken by slicing horizontally without cutting all the way through and open up like a book.
- Lay the chicken out on pieces of cling film and sprinkle with salt and pepper.
- Place the leeks and mushrooms along the breast and roll up into a sausage. Then roll in cling film, twist both ends and tie in a knot.
- Heat the chicken stock in a shallow pan, submerge the cling filmed chicken and poach for 8–10 minutes.
- Bring the vinegar up to boil, add the shallots and cook until soft – set aside to cool.
- Then mix the cooled vinegar with the tomatoes and the chopped herbs.
- When ready to serve, remove the chicken from the cling film and slice each breast into three with the tomato herb dressing alongside.

- Anton recommends this dish is served with baby market vegetables, see chapter 14.

Wine Recommendation
White Rioja, Sancerre Rosé, Fleurie
or a light New Zealand Pinot Noir

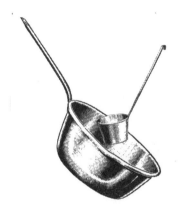

BREAST OF PHEASANT WITH PANCETTA, CHESTNUT AND MUSHROOM

The secret of tender pheasant is to marinate it for as long as possible beforehand and then wrap it in bacon whilst cooking. This recipe combines some lovely Autumnal flavours and would be excellent with the Colcannon and Honey-Roasted Root Vegetables we have described in chapter 14.

INGREDIENTS

6 pheasant breasts
600ml red wine
bay leaf, peppercorns & garlic
  cloves
2 tbsp. olive oil
6 slices of pancetta
30g butter
250g button mushrooms,
  chopped

120g peeled chestnuts,
  crumbled
salt, pepper and brown sugar
  to taste
2 tsp. arrowroot mixed with a
  little cold water
parsley, chopped

METHOD

- Marinate the pheasant with the red wine, bay leaf, peppercorns and garlic for at least 24 hours. Drain and reserve the liquid. Pat the pheasant dry.
- Heat a little oil in a heavy based frying pan and seal the pheasant on each side. Allow them to cool then wrap each breast with a slice of pancetta.
- Place in a roasting tin with approximately ⅓ of the marinade liquid and cook in a hot oven at 220°C for 15–20 minutes.
- Meanwhile, melt the butter in a frying pan and sauté the mushrooms for 2–3 minutes.
- Pour in the remaining marinade, add the chestnuts and bring the mixture to the boil.
- Once the pheasant breasts are cooked, transfer them to a serving dish and 'deglaze' the pan (for those of you now flummoxed – that is a technical culinary term for adding a little cold liquid to a very hot pan or roasting tin in order to melt all the delicious cooking residue and add it to your sauce).

- Thicken the chestnut and mushroom sauce with arrowroot and pour it over the pheasant.
- Sprinkle with chopped parsley.

Wine Recommendations
Chianti Classico, Vacqueyras or Corbieres .

Ye Olde Wattling Restaurant

CANNON OF LAMB STEAMED IN SPINACH

This is the most sensational way to cook delicate, lean, pink lamb. The cannons are steamed within the spinach leaves and totally sealed to retain maximum flavour and moisture.

INGREDIENTS
3 x cannon of lamb
salt and freshly ground black pepper
1 tbsp. olive oil
225g large leaf spinach, washed
2 tbsp. redcurrant jelly

METHOD
- Season the lamb with salt and pepper.
- Heat a little oil in a heavy-based frying pan and seal the lamb on all sides until well browned. Allow to cool.
- Blanch the spinach by plunging into boiling water, transfer to a bowl of iced water to refresh and then drain.
- Lay the spinach leaves out to make 3 rectangles twice the size of the lamb.
- Season the redcurrant jelly with salt and pepper and spread onto the spinach. Place the lamb into the middle and fold the spinach over completely encasing the meat.
- Place onto a greased baking sheet, cover with greaseproof paper and seal with tin foil. Cook in the oven at 200°C for 12–15 minutes.
- When cooked, allow to rest for a few minutes then cut each log of lamb into 6 slices and arrange 3 per person on individual plates. Serve with the Cumberland or Choron Sauces detailed in chapter 15.

Wine Recommendation
This is a dish worth complimenting with something special.
*Cru Classic Claret, Californian Cabernet/Merlot blends,
or Southern Australia's top Cabernet-Shiraz*

A PARTRIDGE IN A PEAR TREE

I will not try to explain where the inspiration for this dish came from – suffice to say that Pear and Partridge really were created to go together and if you wish to use this recipe for a little themed Christmas fun please do so.

INGREDIENTS

6 x dressed partridge
salt and pepper
150ml white wine
150ml chicken stock
2 large pears

25g butter
25g demerara sugar
125g blueberries
2 tbsp. arrowroot
1 bunch of watercress

METHOD

- Heat a little oil in a frying pan. Season the partridge with salt and pepper and seal in the pan. Remove and place in a deep roasting tin breast side down.
- Pour in the white wine and stock around the birds in the tin and 'French roast' in the oven at 180°C for 20 minutes.
- Remove from the oven, turn the partridge the right side up and then roast again for a further 10–15 minutes until the skin is nicely browned.
- Cut the pears in half, cut out the core then slice into half moon disks.
- Heat the butter and sugar in a frying pan, add the pears and cook gently to caramelise. Add the blueberries and allow them to warm through.
- Once the partridge is cooked, remove from the tin and keep warm. Strain the juices into a saucepan. Mix the arrowroot with a little water to form a runny paste and stir this into the juices to thicken. Season with salt and pepper.
- Surround the partridges with the caramelised pear and blueberry, garnish with sprigs of watercress and serve the sauce separately.

Wine Recommendation
Oregon Pinot Noir, Châteauneuf du Pape
or as it's Christmas, a top Burgundy.

CALVES LIVER, SMOKED BACON AND ONION GRAVY

No City cookbook would be complete without calves liver. At Just Gladwins it remains our single most popular dish all year round. Perhaps this is because no one cooks liver at home any more, so here is a recipe to put that right.

INGREDIENTS FOR 6
700g calves liver, thinly sliced
2 tbsp. seasoned flour
salt and pepper
2 tbsp. olive oil
6 rashers smoked back bacon

FOR ONION GRAVY
25g butter
3 onions, sliced
50ml red wine
50ml chicken stock
1 tbsp. tomato puree
1 lemon, juice only

METHOD FOR THE ONION GRAVY
- Heat the butter in a saucepan and fry the onions for 3–4 minutes until golden.
- Add the red wine and simmer to reduce by half.
- Add the chicken stock, tomato puree and lemon. Season with salt and pepper and bring to the boil.

METHOD FOR CALVES LIVER AND BACON
- Heat the oil in a frying pan until smoking hot. Fry the bacon and transfer to another dish to keep warm.
- Coat the liver in seasoned flour, then chargrill for just 1–2 minutes on each side.
- Serve with the Colcannon, detailed in chapter 14, and the onion gravy.

Wine Recommendations
Almost anything red and a bit fruity:
Rioja, South African Pinotage, Chilean Cabernet

CHAPTER 12

THE BARON OF BEEF

> *"Most turkeys taste better the day after; my Mother's tasted better the day before."* – RITA RUDNER

I had been invited to cook for a small dinner in the crypt of the mighty Guildhall and I clearly remember the day I was first shown around the huge back of house kitchen area. The rather frightening 'Keeper of the Guildhall' pointed out to me the two most enormous ovens I had ever set eyes on. Massive iron structures each larger than most modern kitchens with great cast iron double doors opening to a blackened interior chamber. There was no floor to the ovens in order to provide enough oxygen to burn the five rows of giant gas jets. The only adjustment was a "damper" at the top that would apparently, to some degree, vent and thus reduce the scorching temperature. The Keeper proudly told me that this was where the Barons of Beef were cooked for the great City banquets and then added forcefully that I was not to go anywhere near them. I had my own private moment of pride when some 10 years later I cooked my first Baron for the 1994 Lord Mayor's banquet in those self same ovens.

Alas, those cooking appliances of a bygone age were finally condemned a couple of years ago and had to be cut into pieces with oxyacetylene torches in order to be removed. The great kitchens too, after generations of feasts and banquets, saw their last meal on 31st March 2006 –a humble but nonetheless tasty Lamb Casserole was their swan song before the demolition contractors took over. It will be 2009 before a spanking new 21st Century kitchen appears in its place.

A Baron of Beef is a very large 'saddle' joint comprising two full sirloins left uncut at the backbone. The French Surloigne (above loin) is said to have been renamed after James I, King of England, who knighted this cut of beef because of its superior quality. Taking the joke further, the title Baron being superior to a Sir was adopted for the magnificent double sirloin joint.

Beef is very much the first dish we associate with the City of London, be it business people eating steaks, livery companies serving beef puddings or joints being carved in private dining rooms. The art of fine carving is also something an Englishman takes great pride in and is often assumed to be an expert at. It reminds me of a good friend who, because of his reputation as an excellent carver, was invited by his hostess to take on the role at a large family lunch party. A grand table of 24 eager diners faced him with small children at one end and senior generations at the other. He carefully reshaped his knife and beads of sweat appeared on his forehead as he calculated his task of apportioning the single roast chicken that had been placed before him. Thankfully, before things became too embarrassing the hostess reappeared and asked whether he had finished serving the children and was ready to tackle the beef. There is a lesson here for all of us – give clear instruction and if in doubt, ask.

One of the great patriotic occasions in the City each year is the St George's Day Banquet of the Royal Society of St George. Central to this most traditional event is the presentation and serving of The Roast Beef of Old England. A military brigade of drummers and a procession of chefs carry the Baron of Beef into the dining hall to present it to the Top Table. The Chairman then addresses them:

"I charge you to declare that this beef is fit for the consumption and delight of my guests."

To which the chef is obliged to answer

"I so do".

Bernard Sullivan, the legendary toastmaster in charge of all great City occasions recalls the St George's Day Banquet as having his favourite toast of the year.At the end of the dinner there is always a moving, highly patriotic speech culminating in the toast which is simply:

"ENGLAND."

Not a dry eye in the house.

BEEF WELLINGTON

Unfortunately, or fortunately dependent on your view point, my long established catering company, Party Ingredients, has a reputation for Beef Wellington cooked perfectly pink and carved just before serving. It is a wonderful celebratory dish but just a little stressful for the poor old chef when ordered for 800 guests.

INGREDIENTS FOR 6–8
1–1.5kg beef fillet
salt and pepper
500g block puff pastry
1 egg, salted and lightly
   whisked

MUSHROOM DUXELLES
55g butter
500g field mushrooms, finely
   chopped
1 clove garlic
1 tbsp. finely chopped parsley

METHOD
- Season the beef with salt and pepper. On the hob heat a little oil in a heavy-based roasting tin and sear the fillet on all sides. Immediately transfer to a hot oven and roast for 10 minutes at 220°C.
- Remove the beef from the oven and allow to cool.
- For the duxelles, sweat the garlic and mushrooms in a pan over a low heat then leave to cool. When cold, place the mixture on a tea towel and squeeze out all the juice. Mix in the parsley and season with salt and pepper.
- Roll the pastry out to an even rectangle (not a map of Great Britain) so you can completely wrap the beef in it. Trim to size and save the pastry off-cuts to decorate.
- Spread the duxelle down the centre of the pastry lengthways to the same size as the fillet. Place the beef on top.
- Fold the pastry over the meat and seal with an overlap by brushing with egg.
- Repeat with the ends of the pastry folding them up and sealing.
- Turn the whole parcel over so the joins are on the underside. Cut and score leaves out of the pastry off-cuts and decorate the top of the Wellington. Brush with the rest of the beaten egg then place on a baking sheet lined with baking paper. Refrigerate until ready to cook.

- Cook in a preheated oven at 180°C for 25–30 minutes until golden brown.
- Carve the Wellington at the table and serve with Sauce Bearnaise. See chapter 15.

Smithfield Market

MILK ROASTED LOIN OF PORK WITH HONEY AND MUSTARD

I tease my wife for repeatedly churning this dish out for every large-scale family occasion. The criticism is unfair because it is absolutely mouth watering and has the advantage of holding well if the relatives are late!

INGREDIENTS FOR 6–8
1½–2kg boned and rolled pork loin
salt and pepper
2 cloves garlic
1 lemon
4 tbsp. runny honey
2 tbsp. grainy mustard
1½ pints milk

METHOD
- Cut the garlic into thin slivers, peel the rind off the lemon with a potato peeler and cut into strips.
- Cut small splits across the grain of the pork and slip the garlic and lemon zest into the meat. Season with salt and pepper.
- Place the pork in a deep roasting dish. Mix the honey and mustard together and spoon over.
- Heat the milk to boiling point and then pour around the meat. Roast in the oven uncovered for 2–2½ hours at 160°C.
- Once cooked, allow the meat to rest. Carve and serve with the cooking juices spooned over.

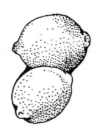

SHANK OF LAMB WITH RED ONION, APRICOT AND PINENUTS

This robust, wholesome winter dish is ideal to prepare well in advance and then reheat or keep warm until needed. For me, very cooked lamb is a completely different meat to pink racks or cannons but every bit as delicious. Here, slow cooking captures all the flavour of the red wine and rosemary in the incredibly tender flesh.

INGREDIENTS FOR 6

6 lamb shanks	2 bunches rosemary
olive oil	1 red onion
salt and pepper	120g dried apricots
1 bottle red wine	60g pinenuts
500ml lamb stock	2 tbsp. arrowroot

METHOD

- Season the lamb with salt and pepper and brown the shanks in a hot frying pan on all sides. Transfer to an ovenproof casserole dish then add the red wine, lamb stock and rosemary, reserving 6 sprigs for garnish. Cover with a lid and cook in the oven at 140°C for 2–2½ hours.
- Thinly slice the onion and the apricots then cook them together in a little olive oil until softened. Season with salt and pepper, add the pinenuts and keep warm.
- When the shanks are cooked, the meat should be nearly falling off the bone. Remove them from the cooking liquid and where the flesh meets the bone at the top, gently pull it away and spoon in the onion stuffing. The shanks can then be kept warm until dinner is served.
- Strain the cooking liquor and bring to the boil. Check the seasoning then mix the arrowroot with a little cold water, add to the sauce and allow it to thicken.
- Garnish the shanks with rosemary sprigs and serve with honey roasted root vegetables. See chapter 14.

ROAST BEEF AND YORKSHIRE PUDDING

What great British cookbook about the City would be complete without Roast Beef and Yorkshires? In France the Brits are even called Ros Bifs and should be proud of it. This recipe forgoes the tradition of serving the puddings and gravy before the beef 'to fill the family up' but nonetheless it is a classic.

INGREDIENTS FOR 6–8
2–2.5kg sirloin of beef (on the bone)
salt and pepper

FOR THE YORKSHIRE PUDDING	FOR THE GRAVY
115g flour	meat juices
1 egg	2 tbsp. plain flour
200ml milk	550ml vegetable stock
100ml water	salt and pepper
salt	mustard
60g lard	horseradish sauce
	1 tbsp. treacle

METHOD FOR BEEF
- Place the beef in a roasting tin and season with salt and pepper.
- Put in a preheated oven at 240°C for 20 minutes then turn down the heat to 190°C and cook for 15 minutes per ½kg for rare beef, and extra 15 minutes for medium rare and a further 30 minutes for well done.
- Remove from the oven and allow to rest for at least 15 minutes before carving.

METHOD FOR THE YORKSHIRE PUDDING
- The Yorkshire pudding mixture can be made in advance and left to stand for 1 hour. Place the flour in a food processor. Mix the egg, milk and water together and pour into the food processor via the funnel with the motor on to produce a smooth batter. Season with salt.
- Heat the lard until searing hot in 12 individual or 2 large tins. Pour the batter on top and bake in the oven at 200°C. Individuals 15–20 minutes. Large ones 30 minutes.

METHOD FOR GRAVY

- To make a simple gravy once the meat is cooked remove it to a separate dish and place the roasting tin on the hob. Stir in the flour and cook for a couple of minutes stirring to a smooth paste.
- Gradually add the vegetable stock and continue stirring. Season to taste with salt, pepper, mustard, horseradish and black treacle.

CORN-FED CHICKEN INFUSED WITH ORANGE AND ROSEMARY

A recipe introduced to us by a delightful old colonel when he was the learned Clerk of The Society of Apothecaries in Blackfriars. Thirty years in the catering corps he was a fountain of culinary knowledge, fussy as hell and an honour to have served. This one is yours Colonel Stinger.

INGREDIENTS FOR 4–6
1 x 2–2½kg corn-fed chicken
2 oranges
1 bunch rosemary
1 dstsp. olive oil
salt and pepper
200ml chicken stock
200ml white wine

METHOD
- Take one of the oranges and half the rosemary and use it to stuff into the cavity of the chicken.
- Gently loosen the skin from around the breast of the chicken and slide the remaining rosemary under it.
- Smear the chicken with the olive oil, salt and pepper and place in a deep roasting tin. Pour the white wine, chicken stock and the juice from the remaining orange into the base of the tin. Roast in the oven at 200°C for about 1½ hours.
- When cooked lift out the chicken, draining any juices in the cavity back into the pan. Transfer the bird to a carving board, cover it well and allow to rest for 15 minutes.
- Skim off any excess fat from the cooking liquid, bring it to the boil then strain into a jug.
- Carve the chicken at the table and spoon over the juices.

CHAPTER 13

A WILD BOAR IN THE HEART OF THE CITY

The City of London is a remarkable place. It can boast having a "Chief Commoner" – presumably someone voted by the populous as having the best cockney accent using the most colourful language. Or "The Recorder of London". Is this a man with one of those long fluffy microphones standing on the busy junction outside Bank tube recording traffic noise? Why not then a "Head Bore" – the person captained as leader by those dreadful bores we have all come across at City dinners. One's imagination can run riot with the idea of rival candidates sitting at long polished dining tables each going on and on with never ending tales, always centred around themselves and never quite achieving a conclusion or punch line.

The Boar's Head on the other hand is quite another matter. Originally the Nordic God Fey, who watched over crops and livestock, was symbolised by a wild boar.The boar was sacrificed in the hope of securing a prosperous Spring herd. As Christianity took over, pagan customs were often incorporated and the presentation of a boar's head became a Christmas tradition. The increased scarcity of Wild Boar, however, has meant that this ceremony has largely died away and been forgotten except in a couple of obscure corners of the City.

On a chilly December afternoon in St Bartholomew's Close behind Bart's hospital, a group of robed gentlemen, soldiers, military drum corp and mounted police escort assemble to parade a fanciful bright red representation of a huge boar's head through the City of London. To the astonishment and amusement of passers by clicking photos with their mobile phones, The Butchers' Company are repeating a 650 year old ceremony of presenting a boar's head to the Lord Mayor, in return for being permitted in 1343 to purchase a parcel of land near Fleet Street to slaughter their beasts. On arrival at the Mansion House the false head is replaced by a fully fledged stuffed one and the Lord Mayor and assembled company partake in small slices – how's that for a Christmas present!

I requested a recipe from The Butchers' Company with the idea of including it as a classic in this book. The document which arrived covering the cutting from the carcass, draining, brining, precise detail on de-boning (leaving, of course, the nose bone and chin skin), stuffing, bandaging, binding the ears inserted with carrots, braising, then finally intricately decorating – was magnificent, but regrettably I felt you the reader were unlikely to try it at home.

The Cutlers' Company also celebrate Christmas 'the old fashioned way' and hold an annual Boar's Head Feast. Here, at their banquet an ornate stuffed boar's head is presented as the course after the main at a banquet. Two chefs parade the head on a stretcher accompanied by a young page carrying the mustard pot, trumpeters, soldiers and choristers singing the Boar's Head carol. The head chorister is rewarded with the presentation of an orange (another great Christmas present) and the lucky Master Cutler is served a small sample slice of the head. Hereafter, the enjoyment of the feast is allowed to take over from tradition and a suitable 'Wild Boar' savoury course is served to the whole company. For example, Terrine of Wild Boar with Spiced Apricots or Crispy Boar Salad with Black Truffle.

Modern British cooking today, with the possible exception of Boar's Head, has provided wonderful interpretations of classic dishes and there are some very talented chefs in the City who have contributed these stunning 'classic' recipes:

> *"If the English can survive their food, they can survive anything."*
> – *GEORGE BERNARD SHAW*

CHARLIE BOYD'S OXTAIL STEW

Charles Boyd is a born and bred City chef – Butchers Hall, Mansion House, Guildhall, The HAC, he has cooked in them all and over the years has established a highly successful catering company. It is always good to know when other people do things better than you and I was really pleased when Charlie contributed this classic oxtail recipe to our City collection.

INGREDIENTS

2 oxtails, cleaned and cut into portions
seasoned flour
30g beef dripping
500g carrots and onions cut into cubes
150ml red wine
570ml beef stock
salt and pepper
½ tsp. sugar
sprig of fresh thyme, chopped
1 tsp. tomato puree
juice of ½ lemon

METHOD

* Coat the oxtails in seasoned flour.
* Heat the beef dripping in a large heavy pan, then brown the tails, one piece at a time, on all sides.
* Fry off the carrots and onions and add to the oxtail, pour over the red wine, beef stock, salt, pepper, sugar and thyme and bring to the boil.
* Simmer for 1 hour skimming off the sediment from time to time.(Charlie called it 'skimming the scum' but I thought that might totally put you off trying the recipe.)
* Remove the meat and vegetables into a casserole dish.
* Add the tomato puree and lemon juice to the cooking liquor and reduce by about a third.
* Pour the reduced liquor over the meat and vegetables and cook in the oven for 2 hours until the meat is melt-in-the-mouth tender.
* Serve the stew with Horseradish Mash and garnish with Parsnip Crisps (see chapter 14 for recipes).

WILD BOAR CHOPS WITH CARAMELISED APPLE AND ROQUEFORT

Despite my derogatory remarks about cooking the Boar's Heads, wild boar is a fabulous robust meat which works well with other strong flavours such as this Roquefort Butter. You may have to shop around a bit to find boar but if not, this recipe will do perfectly well with pork chops.

INGREDIENTS FOR 6	ROQUEFORT BUTTER
6 wild boar chops	1 onion
salt and pepper	225g unsalted butter
2 cox's apples	115g Roquefort cheese
15g butter 1 tbsp.	2 tbsp. chives, finely chopped
soft brown sugar	salt and pepper

METHOD FOR ROQUEFORT BUTTER
- Finely dice the onion and fry gently until soft in a little bit of the unsalted butter. Leave to get completely cold.
- Soften the remaining butter and crumble in the Roquefort then add the cooked onion and beat all three things together. Season with salt and pepper and chopped chives.
- Roll the Roquefort butter into a 5cm diameter log, wrap in cling film and chill until needed.

METHOD FOR CHOPS
- Season the chops with salt and pepper and seal on both sides in a heavy-based frying pan with a little bit of oil. Transfer to a baking tray and bake in the oven at 200°C for 20 minutes.
- Whilst the chops are cooking, cut each apple into 3 discs taking out the core. Then fry them in butter and a little sugar until caramelised.
- Top the chops with a disc of apple, a slice of chilled Roquefort Butter and flash under a hot grill until the butter starts to melt. Serve with its own juices.

TERENCE CONRAN'S STEAK AND KIDNEY PUDDING

An old City staple – rich, satisfying and the perfect match for robust heavy red wine.

INGREDIENTS FOR 6–8
1.5kg chuck steak, diced 1″ cubes
100g flour
1 onion, sliced
100ml Guinness
30ml Worcestershire sauce
1 bay leaf and thyme
500ml beef stock
700g ox kidney, diced, core removed

SUET PASTRY
500g plain flour
250g suet
1 tsp. baking powder
a pinch of salt
2 eggs, beaten
cold water

METHOD
- Roll the steak in seasoned flour, sear in a hot frying pan until brown on all sides then transfer to a deep baking tin.
- Heat the onion, Guinness, and Worcester Sauce in a pan and boil to reduce by two thirds.
- Pour the reduced mixture over the meat then add the bay leaf, thyme and stock. Cover with a lid or foil and place in the oven at 150°C.
- Place the kidneys in a pan, cover with water and bring to the boil.Pour off the water and leave kidneys to one side.
- When the steak has been cooking for 1½ hours add the kidneys to the mixture and cook for a further 1½ hours until tender. Remove steak and kidney mix from the oven and chill.

FOR THE PASTRY
- Place dry ingredients in a mixing bowl, add the eggs and cold water to form a dough.
- Divide pastry into 2 balls, one twice the size of the other and roll out into circles 6mm thick.
- Grease a china pudding bowl then line it with the larger disc of pastry. Spoon in the meats, top up with gravy – saving the excess gravy to serve separately.

- Lay the other disc of pastry over the top and pinch the pastry lid and base together to seal.
- Cover with oiled greaseproof paper, tied securely with string and steam in a pan of water for 2 hours then serve.

NB. The pan must not boil dry!

NEARLY NO.1 LOMBARD STREET'S COQ AU VIN

Dining at Herbert Berger's No.1 Lombard Street restaurant is all about attention to detail and quality. Why then was I surprised when his famous Coq Au Vin recipe arrived as a multi-page document? I apologise to all, but to fit it in the book I have had to trim and edit. Herbert's key tips however, remain – use a top rate chicken, buy an expensive bottle of wine (you will taste the difference) and allow 3 days to make it.

INGREDIENTS FOR 4–6
1 large free range chicken (black leg, organic or bresse) jointed into 8

MARINADE	GARNISH
1 bottle of good burgundy	150g smoked streaky bacon,
1 onion	cut into lardons
1 carrot	50g small button mushrooms
some leek, celeriac and	12 small button mushrooms
celery chopped	(peeled and cooked)
stalks from mushrooms	50g butter maldon salt, pepper
½ bulb garlic	oil for frying
1 bay leaf, thyme and	parsley
peppercorns	
¼ litre veal stock	
½ tsp. arrowroot	

METHOD
- Mix all the marinade ingredients, pour over the chicken pieces and leave in fridge for 36 to 48 hours.
- Drain the chicken and separate from the vegetables. Keep the wine separately. Pat the chicken dry.
- Heat the oil in a casserole dish, season the chicken and fry until nicely browned. Set aside.
- Now fry the marinated vegetables until transparent. Add the wine to the pan, bring to the boil and reduce by half.

- Add the chicken pieces and veal stock. Cover with a lid – cook in the oven at 130°C for 45 minutes.
- Remove chicken to serving dish. Bring the sauce to the boil and again reduce by half. Thicken the sauce with arrowroot.
- Fry the bacon and mushrooms together, then sprinkle over the chicken, followed by the sauce and chopped parsley.

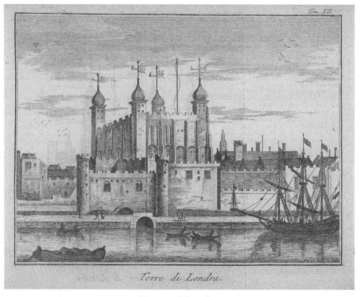

Tower of London

RACK OF VENISON WITH RED ONION MARMALADE

Thanks to deer farming, venison is now much more readily available and you should not have to go too far to find these sumptuous lean racks. Venison must be served rare as it will get sinewy and tough with over-cooking.

INGREDIENTS FOR 4–6
1 rack venison (8 bone)
salt and pepper
600ml game stock
200ml red wine
1 small glass of port
2 tbsp. black treacle
¼ tsp. mixed spice
2 tbsp. arrowroot

ONION MARMALADE
15g butter
2 red onions, thinly sliced
2 tbsp. seville orange
   marmalade
1 tbsp. sherry vinegar

METHOD FOR ONION MARMALADE
- Heat the butter in a heavy-bottomed frying pan, and cook the onions until they are soft. Add the sherry vinegar and orange marmalade. Cook gently for 10 minutes until the liquid has evaporated and the onions are very soft.

METHOD
- Season the venison with salt and pepper. Heat some oil in a large heavy-based frying pan and sear the venison rack on all sides until nicely browned.
- Place the venison in a roasting tin, then mix together the stock (if you do not have game, a chicken stock will do), wine, port, treacle and mixed spice then pour it around the rack.
- Cook in the oven at 200°C for 25 minutes.
- Once the meat is cooked, transfer it to another dish and keep warm. Strain the cooking liquid into a small pan and bring to the boil. Check the flavour and adjust the seasoning then mix the arrowroot with a little cold water and add it to the jus to thicken.
- Carve the venison into cutlets and serve with the jus and marmalade.

CHAPTER 14

GOING TO MARKET

"I do not like broccoli. And I haven't liked it since I was a little kid and my mother made me eat it. And I'm President of the United States and I'm not going to eat any more broccoli." – GEORGE BUSH

One of the few perks I can think of for being a chef is that you can justify travelling abroad as necessary research to broaden culinary horizons. As well as working in France and Switzerland (both a very long time ago), I have been fortunate enough to have made 'foodie' trips right across the world and in any new country I make a point of visiting the local food markets. In order to learn more about Thai food I went to Bangkok with a dear friend and Thai chef – Chai Thittichai (I should probably have asked him for a recipe for this book but he was not very City). Markets in places like Thailand are as much about eating as purchasing and the mixture of street cooking, produce sampling, bartering and interaction was over-whelming, together with the widest range of exotic produce you could imagine. Deep-fried grasshoppers in a choice of grades and sizes ready to munch there and then or take home. Incredibly smelly darian fruit – a delicacy and somewhat acquired taste to which a Westerner's reaction entertains stall holders for hours.

Sao Paulo in Brazil was something else. Olivia Stewart-Cox and I were flown out at the time of the Queen's Golden Jubilee to help promote British produce to the Brazilian market. Little did we know that on arrival I would be on the front page of a national newspaper and a TV news team would follow us wherever we went. We were equipped with a large, very friendly team of willing but somewhat 'mañana' chefs and launched into a non-stop programme of cookery demonstrations, interviews, TV appearances and parties to both cook for and present. Our brigade's lack of English and our total lack of Portuguese led to some hilarious moments, but that is for another book – the point of this story is markets that I insisted we should visit.

Fish was indoors against the scorching heat and we watched small swarthy fishmongers skillfully filleting pilchard-type fish with a single stroke of a very, very sharp blade. For the benefit of the cameras I foolishly joined in and was quickly put to shame. At the fruit market the pineapple shed alone was the size of a Heathrow terminal piled high with thousands upon thousands of the fruits. Now with an entourage of small children in tow we were creating quite a commotion and rival traders were vying to present us with samples. Finally the meat markets, where the sheer quantities of prime beef contrasted so dramatically with the horrendous poverty of this enormous city's slums. So much for promoting food from Britain, we were gobsmacked by food from Brazil.

Returning to our London markets I am always delighted to note that market banter and friendliness is still as prevalent here at home if a little less excitable. It seems to me that the world over traders in fresh produce are enthused by their product, inspired by what a chef might do with it and clearly well fed themselves. The City markets Billingsgate, Smithfield and Spitalfields are all no exception.

How a cockney youth can be so 'chipper' about a load of wet fish at 4 o'clock in the morning is beyond me and yet throughout Billingsgate that is how they are. The market itself is now situated at Trafalgar Way outside the square mile but all 3 City markets are still managed by the City of London Corporation. For over 600 years Billingsgate market was along the Thames waterside and it started life trading in coal, corn, iron, wine, salt and pottery as well as fish. Since the 16th Century, however, it has specialised in fish alone.

Smithfield is the oldest London market, still situated on meadows where beasts were brought for slaughter as early as the 10th Century. When I recently met a leading trader he was fiercely proud of his market's heritage and place in the City. Criticism of the 120 year old buildings was dismissed. There has recently been a major internal modernisation and today Smithfield trades in a huge range of products and specialist breeds etc. not just from Britain but from all over the world. The quaint Victorian setting is part of our history – long may it be preserved.

Spitalfields, like Billingsgate, has surrendered to relocation to a vast 31 acre site in the East End. Visiting a fruit and vegetable market always gives me the same feelings of heightened senses and elation. It is the combination of smells, the bustle and visual rainbow of colour – fruits, flowers and vegetables all grown somewhere by loving hands and hard work to come to market and fulfil their destiny. This market has a mere 300 year history – prior to that the grower of a turnip or an apple would sell it locally or eat it themselves.

Now what, you may ask, has happened to the old Spitalfields and Billingsgate market buildings? Well, for a while at least they have been given over to a brand new City trade – the phenomena of the corporate staff party. When in 1991 Spitalfields first moved out of its splendid Victorian halls, it left a vast empty indoor space too tempting for entrepreneurial event organisers to resist adopting for elaborate office parties. We are not talking about buying a few bottles of cheap fizz, some packets of crisps and doing something disgusting on the office photocopier. This was the beginning of major themed extravaganzas often for over a thousand guests, designed to demonstrate a corporation's wealth as well as generosity. Big tops with circus performers, Treasure Islands or Star Wars all with lavish seated dinners, cocktail bars, indoor funfair, live bands and entertainment. Spitalfields eventually closed its doors to this to be redeveloped but the activity had spread to other locations. The even more impressive Old Billingsgate Buildings have taken up the mantle hosting hugely expensive hospitality events, awards ceremonies and parties. Thankfully the smell of fish has disappeared. I think it is fair to say there is always a place in the market and let's return to those glorious fresh vegetables and my romantic notion that they were grown especially for you.

ANTON'S MEDLEY OF BABY MARKET VEGETABLES

The availability of tender sweet vegetables is now excellent and they make a really stylish accompaniment to main course dishes.

INGREDIENTS FOR 6
12 baby carrots
6 baby courgettes split lengthways
12 baby leeks trimmed to 10cm
6 small broccoli florets
maldon salt
freshly ground black pepper
melted butter

METHOD
* Blanch the vegetables individually in salted boiling water.
* Toss in a little melted butter and season with maldon salt and freshly ground black pepper.

HORSERADISH AND TOASTED WALNUT MASH

Charles Boyd's perfect accompaniment to Oxtail Stew, see chapter 13.

INGREDIENTS FOR 6–8
900g desiree potatoes
180g butter
150ml créme fraîche
salt and pepper
1 level tsp. fresh grated horseradish
200g walnuts, chopped

METHOD
* Peel and boil the potatoes in salted water until soft.
* Drain and return to the pan.
* Add the butter, créme fraîche, salt and pepper and combine well to make a smooth mash.
* Stir in the horseradish and walnuts.

ANTONY WORRALL THOMPSON'S VEGETABLES

Innovative and exciting vegetables can give you the opportunity to serve totally plain grilled or poached meat or fish. This is often the very best way and Antony's work on presenting Saturday Kitchen has led him to create some stunning vegetable recipes – here are two of them.

GINGERED CARROTS

INGREDIENTS FOR 6

700g baby carrots
2 oranges
2 tbsp. runny honey
55g unsalted butter
1 tsp. grated ginger

2 tbsp. crystallised ginger, chopped
1 tbsp. chives, chopped
salt and pepper

METHOD

- In a saucepan, place the carrots, juice and zest of the oranges, honey, butter, grated ginger then add enough water to cover the carrots.
- Bring to the boil and cook for approximately 10 minutes until tender.
- Add the crystallised ginger and cook over a high heat until the liquid has almost evaporated, stirring from time to time.
- Add the chives and season to taste. The carrots will have a wonderful glaze.

FRESH PEAS, SPRING ONION AND ARTICHOKES

INGREDIENTS FOR 6

100ml extra virgin olive oil
4 cloves garlic, sliced
6 spring onions, cut into 1
  inch pieces
1 tbsp. thyme leaves, chopped

8 artichoke hearts, tinned
350g freshly podded peas
juice ½ lemon
grated rind 1 lemon
4 tbsp. parsley, chopped

METHOD

- Heat the olive oil in a large saucepan, add garlic and spring onions and cook over a medium heat for approximately 6 minutes until the onions have softened.
- Add the thyme, artichokes, peas and lemon juice. Cook for a further 12 minutes.
- Stir in the lemon rind and parsley. Season to taste.

Leadenhall Market

ASPARAGUS AND BEAN BUNDLES

A well known professional device is to tie vegetables into neat individual portions with ribbons of leek – so why not try it at home.

INGREDIENTS
36 French beans
18 thin asparagus spears
1 leek
a little butter

METHOD
- Trim the ends of the beans and cut the asparagus to the same length.
- Cook in boiling salted water until tender. Remove and refresh under the cold tap.
- Cut the leek lengthways into long ribbons, 1 cm thick and plunge into boiling water for about a minute. Remove and drain.
- Arrange the vegetables into bundles: 6 beans and 3 asparagus spears then bind and tie each bundle with a strip of leek.
- Place the bundles on a buttered baking sheet, cover with greaseproof paper and foil. Reheat in the oven 5 minutes before serving.

HONEY ROASTED ROOT VEGETABLES

A delicious Winter medley – so easy to do and always very well received.

INGREDIENTS FOR 6
3 parsnips
3 carrots
1 medium turnip
50g margarine

2 tbsp. runny honey
2 tbsp. thyme leaves
salt and pepper

METHOD
- Peel and cut all the vegetables into even sized chunks.
- Place in an ovenproof dish with knobs of margarine, honey, thyme, salt and pepper.
- Cook in a hot oven at 220°C for 30–40 minutes, turning once.

KEN LIVINGSTONE'S ROAST NEW POTATOES WITH THYME

We were delighted when Ken Livingstone gave us a contribution for this book. Perhaps making a point that among a catalogue of great City feasts and extravagance, his favourite dish is a roast potato!

INGREDIENTS FOR 6
1kg small new potatoes
60ml olive oil
salt and freshly ground black pepper
1 packet of fresh thyme

METHOD
- Preheat the oven to gas mark 6, 200°C.
- Parboil the potatoes in salted water from 10 minutes. Drain.
- Place the potatoes in a large, shallow roasting pan. Drizzle the olive oil over them, season with plenty of salt and pepper and toss them well to coat.
- Roast the potatoes for 30–40 minutes, or until golden brown and cooked through.
- Pull off the leaves from the sprigs of thyme and toss them with the hot roasted potatoes.
- Serve at once.

PARSNIP AND OTHER CRISPS

Vegetable crisps of all sorts have become very fashionable as both snacks and garnishes. You can try raw beetroot, squash, turnip, swede or even a colourful mixture.

INGREDIENTS F OR 4–6
2 parsnips – peeled
oil for frying
maldon salt

METHOD
- Use a wide-blade vegetable peeler to peel wafer thin lengths of parsnip as long as possible.
- Deep fry in clean oil.
- Drain onto kitchen paper and sprinkle with salt.

COLCANNON

An Irish vegetable mix that I find irresistible with Braised Lamb. It is also excellent with many other casseroles and rustic foods.

INGREDIENTS FOR 6–8
500g peeled old potatoes, maris piper
110g butter, melted
400g savoy cabbage, chopped
240g leeks, finely chopped
200ml double cream
salt and pepper
chopped parsley

METHOD
- Dice the potatoes and cook in boiling salted water until tender
- Drain and then mash with butter.
- In a separate pan cook the cabbage and leeks until soft. Drain well and then mix in with the mashed potato.
- Add the cream to give a moist consistency, season with salt and pepper. Garnish with chopped parsley.

CELERIAC AND APPLE PUREE

There are so many lovely purees that will lift the simplest of meals. Carrot and orange, swede and caraway seeds, broccoli with ground almonds are all delicious and this Celeriac with Apple is no exception.

INGREDIENTS FOR 6–8
600g celeriac, peeled and diced
300g potatoes, maris piper, peeled and diced
1 medium cooking apple
50g butter
100g crème fraîche
celery salt and pepper
parsley, chopped

Method
- Cook the celeriac and potatoes in separate pans of boiling salted water for 20–25 minutes until tender. Drain well.
- Meanwhile, peel and chop the apples and sweat them in a pan with a little water and butter until they are soft and mushy.
- Mash the celeriac, potato and apple together. Add the crème fraîche and season with celery salt and pepper.
- Garnish with chopped parsley.

CHAPTER 15

BRIDGES FOR SALE : SAUCES UNKNOWN

There have certainly been some great marketing coupes in the City of London. The sale of London Bridge to Lake Havasu in Arizona was the ultimate bricks and mortar hustle. With sources to provide inside knowledge of availability and having seen pictures of the Thames running through the City the eager buyers clearly did not bother with the 'show round' when they thought they had purchased the magnificent 1894 opening steel Tower Bridge.

Instead, transported to America and reconstructed stone by stone was the rather dull 1831 London Bridge. It was not even the original London Bridge that was lined with City taverns, shops and houses of ill repute right across the span of the river.

Tower Bridge itself remains standing proud in London adjacent to the tower. It still opens for high masted river traffic to access the City and across the span of it is a room that can now be hired for corporate entertaining and parties. I hasten to add it is the upper span I am talking about; it would be most unfortunate if diners, tucking into their Filet Mignons, were suddenly subjected to an ever increasing tilt and eventual slide into chaos as the bridge open. The downside to catering on this bridge is that there is absolutely no vehicle access. Food, drinks and every plate, glass and fork has to be carried or trolleyed from the south side of the river, along the heavy trafficked road. So if you experience a little grit in your gateau or the bouquet of exhaust fumes in your fumé – don't blame us. The location itself may be a little heavy on the steel but the top of Tower Bridge is really a wonderful place to take visitors to London, looking down on to Tower Hill across the sky-line of the City and up the river to all the other bridges that run across it.

My own Just the Bridge is a restaurant built on the riverside walkway adjacent to the Millennium footbridge and directly opposite Tate Modern. This was to be our City coupe; a swift decision and unique opportunity to take over a bankrupt restaurant and bar premises just weeks before the opening of London's permanent tribute to the new Millennium. There followed a costly but speedy new interior design completed with only days to spare, creation of special menus including such delicacies as *The Millennium Seafood Platter* or *The Shaft of Light Across the Water Cocktail* and recruitment of a mighty new team of maitre d's, chefs, waitresses and support staff ready to greet the masses. We opened 3 days before the fateful Sunday of the initial wobble and the following week, the by now world famous 'wobbly bridge' was closed for restructuring. Our New Millennium Soufflés were left half risen, our Bridge Lobster half steamed, our sauces half thickened and our disappointed team left stranded in a quiet backwater of the City, gazing out across the river to the unreachable Globe Theatre, Tate and tourist filled Southbank on the other side.

It wasn't perhaps that bad but it makes a good story and leads us nicely on to the source of all good cooking – the sauce itself. The following recipes are all very easy to make, hugely versatile and will expand your cooking repertoire no end.

Old London Bridge

HOLLANDAISE

The sauce of Holland is a wonderful thing – it adds richness and flavour to so many otherwise bland dishes and keeps well in the fridge, ready for instant use. This easy to make base recipe is ideal to serve with salmon, asparagus, eggs or spinach. Below are some other derivatives together with their recommended partners.

INGREDIENTS (MAKES 300ML)
6 tbsp. white wine vinegar
8 egg yolks
2 tsp. dijon mustard
salt and freshly ground black pepper
225g unsalted butter

METHOD
- Place the vinegar in a small saucepan and boil vigorously to reduce by two thirds.
- Put the egg yolks and mustard in a food processor and blend for about a minute. Season well with salt and freshly ground black pepper.
- Melt the butter in a small saucepan and bring to the boil.
- Add the reduced vinegar to the butter
- Slowly pour the hot butter mixture into the food processor with the blade running. Within a few moments the hollandaise will thicken.

Sauce Dijonnaise –	Add an extra teaspoon of Dijon and 3 teaspoons of whole grain mustard. The ideal companion for steak.
Sauce Bearnaise –	Cook a finely diced shallot in the vinegar and add some chopped chives, chervil and tarragon to the finished sauce. Perfect with white fish, chicken or other fowl.
Sauce Choron –	As Bearnaise but add 2 teaspoons of tomato puree and some finely chopped sun-blushed tomato.Classic with fillet of lamb or beef.

BALSAMIC REDUCTION

This is one of those trade secrets used as a dressing in fancy restaurants to give all sorts of dishes a little of the wow factor. It simply comprises of an inexpensive bottle of balsamic, reduced down then caramelised into a thick syrup. By keeping it in a squeezy bottle, you can add fine black zigzags, spirals or swirls of sweet spicy vinegar to dress up any plate you choose.

INGREDIENTS
500ml of balsamic vinegar
100g sugar

METHOD
- Pour the vinegar into a small saucepan and boil until the liquid has reduced by about a half.
- Add the sugar and continue to cook for a further 5 minutes.
- Allow to cool before transferring the reduction into a squeezy bottle for storage at room temperature and use any time over the next 50 years!

CUMBERLAND SAUCE

The perfect sweet tangy accompaniment to cold meats, roasted lamb, gammon or terrines and pâtés.

INGREDIENTS
1 medium orange
6 tbsp. port
1 small jar redcurrant jelly
½ tsp. English mustard powder (mixed with a little water)

METHOD
- Strip off the orange peel with a potato peeler and cut into strips.
- Place the orange strips into a saucepan with the port, redcurrant jelly and mustard.
- Bring to the boil and reduce down by about half.
- Chill, ready to serve.

SCANDINAVIAN MUSTARD AND DILL SAUCE

The classic partner for gravadlax, this simple relish is a great one to keep a stock of in the fridge. It is handy for all sorts of salads, smoked fishes or vegetarian dishes.

INGREDIENTS FOR 1/3 LITRE

30ml grainy mustard
15ml dijon mustard
1 small bunch of dill
300ml sunflower oil

30ml tarragon vinegar
3 tsp. castor sugar
salt and pepper

METHOD

- Place both the mustards, dill and tarragon vinegar in a food processor and blend together.
- Slowly add the oil so that the sauce emulsifies.
- Add the sugar and season with salt and freshly ground black pepper.

TARRAGON BEURRE BLANC

Good with almost anything from grilled meats, fish or vegetables such as asparagus or artichokes. Try substituting the tarragon for fresh mint to go with lamb or coriander and red chilli to go with seabass.

INGREDIENTS FOR 400ML

300ml crème fraîche
2 tbsp. tarragon vinegar
1 tsp.castor sugar
75g unsalted butter

1 pkt. fresh tarragon, leaves
chopped
salt, freshly ground black
pepper

METHOD

- Heat the crème fraîche, vinegar and sugar in a heat resilient bowl over a pan of boiling water.
- Cut the butter into small cubes, place them in a separate bowl then pour over the crème fraîche, stirring until all the butter has melted.
- Add the fresh tarragon. Season with salt and freshly ground black pepper.
- Serve warm or reheat over a bain marie.

SALSA SALSA

Although not very 'City' the addition of Salsas to our 'modern British cuisine' has opened up a whole world of possibilities. Instant, adaptable, flavoursome, sauces that keep well and can be served with fish, meat, vegetables, almost anything. Here is your starting point, a red one and a green one.

SALSA ROJA

INGREDIENTS FOR 300ML

2 slices of plain white bread	3 tbsp. red wine vinegar
1 can of pimento (drained)	1 tbsp. soft brown sugar
1 small red pepper	1 small bunch chives, chopped
3 ripe plum tomatoes	150ml olive oil
2 tbsp. tomato puree	salt and pepper

METHOD
- Using a food processor, blitz the bread to make breadcrumbs and then process the pimento into a smooth puree.
- Finely dice the red pepper and tomatoes.
- Now place all the ingredients together in a large mixing bowl, season well and beat together to form a salsa.

SALSA VERDI

INGREDIENTS FOR 250ML

3 slices of plain white bread	2 tbsp. white wine vinegar
1 large bunch of parsley	1 tbsp. castor sugar
1 tin anchovies	150ml olive oil
1 small jar capers	salt and pepper

METHOD
- Literally place all the ingredients together in a food processor and blitz them into a tangy green relish.
- The anchovies in this recipe will replace any need to add salt.

CREAM OF HORSERADISH

Why horseradish is the perfect piquant companion for both roast beef and smoked trout I do not understand. But it undoubtedly is and perhaps we should not question this or the greater conundrum of why fermented grape juice goes so superbly with almost anything. It just does!

INGREDIENTS FOR 200ML

15g fresh horseradish
150ml double cream
1 tbsp. white wine vinegar
a pinch of English mustard
   powder

a teaspoon of castor sugar
salt and pepper

METHOD

- Finely grate the horseradish and soak in 2 tbsp. hot water.
- Whip the double cream to soft peaks.
- Drain the horseradish, squeeze out excess moisture then fold it into the cream.
- Add the white wine vinegar, sugar, a pinch of mustard and season to taste.

TARTARE SAUCE

I have included this recipe to give you a simple guide on how to make your own mayonnaise. Commercial mayonnaise (that white, rather sickly jellied substance) is nothing like the real thing and your tartare sauce demands the real McCoy.

INGREDIENTS FOR 500ML

2 egg yolks	2 dstsp. capers
1 tsp. dijon mustard	1 lemon, rind and juice
1 tbsp. white wine vinegar	small bunch of chervil,
300ml sunflower oil	chopped
6 small gherkins	salt and pepper

METHOD

- Whisk the egg yolks, mustard and white wine vinegar in a mixing bowl.
- Add the oil very slowly a few drops at a time to start with. Continue to whisk until all the oil is used and the mixture emulsifies.
- Chop the gherkins and capers quite finely. Stir into the mayonnaise along with the lemon rind, juice and chervil. Season to taste with salt and pepper.

CHAPTER 16

LEGENDS, KINGS, QUEENS AND PRINCES

> *"The dinner was as remarkable for the splendour and completeness of its appointments as the mansion itself, and the company were remarkable for doing it ample justice..."* – *CHARLES DICKENS*

Myths and facts are always intertwined in the history of an ancient City and out of the confusion come traditions, stories, plays and heritage. To quote the Victorian historian, Professor E. A. Freeman:

"We need not believe that all legends are records of facts but the existence of those legends is a very great fact."

This expresses perfectly the wonderful cocktail that makes up the history of the City of London, and there is no better example than the City's most famous and celebrated Lord Mayor – Dick Whittington.

Was poor Dick a humble boy from Gloucestershire who, together with his cat, walked to London to seek his fortune; met the beautiful daughter of a rich merchant (blonde, long-legged and dressed in tights in most pantos I have seen); then eventually made his fortune; married the girl and became Lord Mayor of London three times? Or was he Richard, the son of Sir William Whytyngdone, a nobleman from Gloucestershire who came to London to become a Mercer (trading in valuable silks and cloths, but not tights); served as Lord Mayor three times and left his fortune to establish almshouses, a college, a library and sanitation for the poor of the City? Either way he was clearly a good bloke and did extremely well for all concerned.

To the South of the City, adjacent to Southwark Bridge is the Ward of Vintry including Five Kings' House and the Vintners' Hall. It is

here that in 1363 the Master Vintner is purported to have entertained five kings together to dinner: Edward III King of England, David King of Scotland, John King of France, Walermar III King of Denmark and Amadeus VI King of Cyprus. Sadly, there is no record of what they ate or what delicious beverages the hosts provided. Some sceptics even say that all five Kings were never in England at the same time and no King of Cyprus was ever called Amadeus. All this, however, is just an attempt at spoiling things. There is plenty of evidence of such a unique and splendid gathering taking place and it has been very much part of the Vintners' Company folklore for over 600 years.

We think of our own generation as being much more conserving and nostalgic than previous ones and it is fascinating to learn that in 1935 the Vintners' Company staged an evening to replicate the Five Kings' Dinner by entertaining the Five Princes of the Crown. Here the records are, of course, accurate and transcripts of the speeches quote Edward HRH The Prince of Wales as wittily offering his regret to his uncle, the Master Vintner, The Earl of Althone that, "You seem socially to have lost a little because on this occasion, you have had to content yourselves with inviting me and my four brothers." Later in the evening, the Archbishop of Canterbury is quoted as saying of himself, "What is the Archbishop of Canterbury doing in that company [ ] it exists to promote the sale of wine and judging by this evening, still exists to encourage its consumption." Clearly a good time was had by all.

For those of you in the mood to once again reconstruct a dinner for five kings or five princes – I will leave the guest list up to you – but detailed on the next page are the menu and wines for the 1935 event:

The Feast of the Five Princes
Vintners' Hall
15th May 1935

Caviar Hors d'Oeuvre
Sherry Amontillado

Clear Turtle
Hock Rauenthal Berg, Auslése 1921

Fillets of Spey Trout
Vert Sauce
Cucumber
Champagne Clicquot 1920

Baron of Beef
Lettuce
Baked Potatoes
Claret
Château Latour 1920
Château Beychevelle 1874

Cygnets
Port Wine Sauce
Chipped Potatoes
Asparagus
Butter Sauce
Burgundy Corton Clos du Roi 1919

York Ham
Vanilla Cream and Pineapple
Port Taylor 1875

Chicken Livers on Toast
Strawberries and Cream
Brandy Courvoisier 1887

Coffee

The City of London continues to make legends out of history. On 15th June 2006, the Lord Mayor hosted a luncheon in his official residence, the Mansion House, in honour of HM Queen Elizabeth II's 80th birthday. Now, in 500 years time, who will possibly believe that two chefs came from each province of Her Majesty's kingdom to do battle for supremacy and that the public would be granted the right to vote and select which chefs would cook for this special birthday party. It sounds like a legend already and the final line-up of Richard Corrigan's Irish Smoked Salmon, Byrn Williams' Turbot with Oxtail, Nick Nairn's Roe Venison and Marcus Wareing's Custard Tart were apparently remarkable.

Unfortunately BBC copyright prevents me from giving you the recipes here but the full menu is shown on the next page. As for desserts fit for Kings, Queens or Princes I have given a selection suitable for the grandest summertime birthday. I have also given my own recipe devised to celebrate the Queen's 80th – who knows perhaps Her Majesty will make it for herself on her 81st.

Ridge View Merret Grosvenor Blanc de Blancs 2001
Sussex, England

***

Smoked Salmon with Blinis, Woodland Sorrel and Cress
Te Mata's Woodthorpe Chardonnay 2004
Hawkes Bay, New Zealand

***

Pan-fried Turbot with Cockles and Oxtail

***

Loin of Roe Venison
with Potato Cake, Roast Roots, Creamed Cabbage and
Game Gravy
Château Margaux 1993

***

Custard Tart with Garibaldi Biscuits
Mount Horrocks Cordon Cut Riesling 2005
Clare Valley, Australia

***

Coffee
Petit Fours

ETON MESS WITH SUMMER BERRIES AND KIRSCH

This school boy dessert originated at Eton College and is literally a 'mess' of mashed up berries, meringue and cream. We served a rather more sophisticated version for The Queen Mother's 100th birthday, adding a necklace of small strawberries and raspberries all the way round each individual's plate.

INGREDIENTS FOR 6

3 large egg whites
175g castor sugar
240g strawberries
240g raspberries
480ml double cream

3 tbsp. kirsch
250g raspberries for raspberry coulis
1 tbsp. icing sugar

METHOD FOR MERINGUE
- Place the egg whites into a clean, dry bowl and whisk into stiff peaks.
- Continue whisking, adding the sugar a tablespoon at a time. • Line a baking tray with baking parchment and dollop spoonfuls of the meringue mixture on to the trays.
- Cook in a low oven at 100°C for 2–3 hours. Turn off the oven and leave overnight for the meringue to dry out.

METHOD
- To make the raspberry coulis. Whiz the raspberries in a food processor and then push through a sieve to get rid of any pips. Season to taste with icing sugar.
- Hull the strawberries, reserve a few for decoration and chop the rest into small pieces. Whip the double cream and the kirsch until firm but still floppy.
- At the last moment fold the meringue, chopped strawberries and second quantity of raspberries into the cream.
- Spoon on to serving plates and serve immediately with the raspberry coulis and the extra strawberries.

Wine Recommendation
Undoubtedly Rosé Champagne, preferably Perrier Jouét or Lanson

LAVENDER AND HONEY CRÈME BRÛLÉE

This recipe for Crème Brûlée has the unusual addition of the aromatic flavour of lavender. However, it is highly adaptable and the lavender can be replaced with peaches, raspberries, fresh mint, sweet spices or, of course, the original – vanilla pod.

INGREDIENTS FOR 6
500ml double cream
6 stalks of lavender flowers
6 egg yolks
40g castor sugar (for mix)
2 tbsp. honey
40g castor sugar (for topping)

METHOD
- In a heavy-based saucepan, scald the cream and lavender flowers then leave to infuse for one hour.
- Mix the egg yolks and sugar together in a bowl. Reheat the cream, sieve the lavender and add it to the egg mix along with the honey.
- Set the bowl over a pan of boiling water and stir occasionally whilst it slowly thickens, allow 15–20 minutes.
- Test the mixture on the back of a wooden spoon – it should be thick and not run back together when parted.
- Pour the cream into ramekins or a shallow dish and leave to set in the fridge overnight. Before serving, sprinkle the tops of the brûlée with the 2nd quantity of sugar and place under a hot grill to melt, bubble and brown.

Wine Recommendation
St Croix du Mont, Sauternes or a German Eiswien.

JOSCELINE DIMBLEBY'S PASSION FRUIT AND NECTARINE JELLY WITH ELDERFLOWER

I was delighted when Josceline Dimbleby contributed this light, delicate Summer dessert – it has all the style and simplicity I have always associated with her cookery writing and is a perfect inclusion to lighten up the City fayre.

INGREDIENTS FOR 6
75ml elderflower cordial mixed with 150ml of water
4 level tsp. of powdered gelatine
600ml fresh orange juice – sieved
flesh and seeds of 6 wrinkled passion fruit
2 white or yellow fleshed nectarines thinly cut into half moon slices

METHOD
- Heat about a quarter of the elderflower mix in a saucepan to boiling point. Remove from the heat and sprinkle in the gelatine powder.
- Leave for a couple of minutes to swell, then stir briskly until the gelatine is completely dissolved. Add the remaining elderflower and orange juice and pour the liquid into a bowl. Leave in the fridge for one hour until lightly set.
- Meanwhile, line a two pint jelly mould with nectarine slices closely pressed against the sides.
- Stir the soft set jelly until smooth, then add the passion fruit.
- Carefully spoon the mixture into the mould and refrigerate to set overnight.
- To turn out, briefly lower the mould into a sink of hot water. Place a serving plate on top, turn them over together, then remove the mould.

Wine Recommendation
English Sparkling Wine is now both recognised and fashionable – perfect with English jelly and ice cream.

CINNAMON AND ARMAGNAC ICE CREAM

Emma Spofforth has been making a huge variety of ice creams for our various catering outlets for more years than I can remember or she cares to tell. No churning, no ice cream maker, no transferring to and from the freezer – just a good electric mixer and some very fattening ingredients.

INGREDIENTS FOR 6–8
6 egg yolks
150g castor sugar
50ml liquid glucose
180ml milk
2 tbsp. Armagnac
1 tsp. cinnamon
500ml dbl. cream

METHOD
- Beat the egg yolks, sugar and liquid glucose together with an electric mixer until pale and fluffy and doubled in volume.
- Scald the milk in a pan and pour slowly into the egg and sugar mixture, beating continuously. Beat for a further 5–10 minutes.
- Whip the cream until stiff then add the Armagnac and Cinnamon to it. Fold the cream and the egg mixture together.
- Transfer to a container or serving dish and freeze overnight.

Wine Recommendation
Inniskillin from Ontario, Canada
Brown Brothers Riesling from Victoria, Australia
or Bonny Doon Muscat from Santa Cruz, California

THE QUEEN'S 80TH BIRTHDAY DESSERT

Sadly they did not invite me to cook for the Queen on her 80th despite all my previous efforts. However, this for me is the perfect royal June dessert – A Crown of Iced English Summer Fruits drizzled with Hot White Chocolate Sauce.

INGREDIENTS FOR 6
400 g raspberries
125 g blueberries
2 ripe peaches stoned and
  sliced
250 g fresh cherries-
  halved and stoned
Icing sugar to dust

INGREDIENTS FOR WHITE CHOCOLATE SAUCE
200ml milk
80ml double cream
½ vanilla pod
2 egg yolks
2 tablespoons caster sugar
1 tspoon cornflour
130g white chocolate buttons

METHOD FOR CHOCOLATE SAUCE
- Heat the milk, cream and vanilla in a pan and bring up to scalding point
- In a bowl mix egg yolks, cornflour and sugar
- Add the egg mix to the milk and stir over a gentle heat until it thickens
- Remove from the heat and stir in the white chocolate until melted.

METHOD
- Choose six presentation dessert plates and carefully arrange a 12cm diameter ring of alternate Raspberries and Blueberries (the jewels around the crown).
- Fill the centre of the ring with a mixture of cherries, peaches and the remaining berries. Then dust with icing sugar
- Stack the plates carefully in the freezer (using an upturned bowl over the fruits to protect them
- Freeze overnight
- 20 minutes before serving remove the fruits from the freezer and allow to semi defrost
- Reheat the white chocolate sauce and drizzle over berries just before serving. Yummy.

CHAPTER 17

THE LORD MAYOR'S PUDDING

"I love long life better than figs." – WILLIAM SHAKESPEARE

Unlike my good friend Ken Livingstone (we have been close ever since he very kindly contributed a new potato to this book), The Lord Mayor of London changes every year with a different Alderman of the City taking office at the beginning of each November. The new Lord Mayor begins his year with a tremendous display of pagentry, ceremony and hospitality including the famous Lord Mayor's Show, The Lord Mayor's Banquet and the slightly lesser known Lord Mayor's Pudding.

Things begin with a discrete private hand-over known as the Silent Ceremony held on a Friday afternoon at precisely 3pm in the Guildhall. The following morning, the Lord Mayor and his entourage go in procession to the Royal Courts of Justice in order to promise to perform the duties of Mayor of the City of London before the Lord Chief Justice and at the same time claim the City's ancient right to do what it damn well likes within the square mile.

This cold November Saturday, usually with a light drizzle falling, is to be spent largely out of doors. The Lord Mayor, Alderman, Sheriffs and all City big wigs dressed up in their fur-lined robes of office meet in the crypt of Guildhall for a breakfast to set them up for the day. Kidneys, bacon, sausages, black pudding, eggs, plenty of mulled wine and the curious additions of fruit cake, soup and scones are all served before they set out in horse drawn carriages to parade through the City streets.

From the 15th to the 19th Century, the procession took place on both land and by river along the Thames, but since 1867 it goes by road alone. Crowds of over half a million people line the route to cheer a splendid array of military bands, themed floats (still called floats from the time the show was on water), elegant open carriages and finally the sumptuous golden coach (built for just this purpose in 1757). The Lord Mayor enthusiastically stretches out of the window to 'present himself to the people of the City' secretly wishing he had resisted that extra sausage at the breakfast. The show day ends with a magnificent firework display on the river by Blackfriars and the new Mayoralty has been launched.

Lord Mayor's Coach outside Mansion House

The following Monday is the day of the Lord Mayors Banquet – one of the nation's greatest civic occasions when with grandiose pomp and ceremony the new Lord Mayor entertains the great and the good to an extravagant multi-course banquet. Records show that in 1555 the Mayor and Sheriffs were granted the princely sum £100 from the City coffers to put on a 'Great and Sumptuous Feast'. Some 80 years later, for the 1634 Banquet, there is a well documented bill of fayre to include: 'pullets, pheasants, partridges, larks, swan, turkey, hare, capon, carp, venison pasty, cold tongue pie, fresh salmons, lobsters, jelly, oringadoe pie, almond leach, preserved tart and marzipan.'

Entrance to dinner is heralded by trumpeters and principal guests are escorted by a body of ancient pikemen. A full orchestra plays as guests are presented with course after course and wine after wine. Until very recently an entree main course (not the American misused term for a starter) as well as a game main course was served. My first Lord Mayor's Banquet was as follows:

THE LORD MAYOR'S BANQUET
Monday, 14th November 1994

Mosaic of Salmon and Halibut
Tarragon Butter Sauce
Chassagne Montrachet 1989

* * *

Baron of Scottish Beef
Miniature Jacket Potatoes with Celeriac and Apple Purée
Roquet Salad with Woodland Mushrooms
Gevry Chambertin Clos Tamisot 1990

* * *

Elderflower Sorbet

* * *

Roast English Partridge
Redcurrant and Wild Rice Stuffing
Bordeaux Wine Sauce
Game Chips and Bread Sauce
Purée of Carrot with Orange
Mangetout
Château Grand-Puy Ducasse 1986

* * *

Trinity Crème Brûlée
Red Fruit Kissel
Domaine de Cantegrit Ste-Croix-du-Mont 1989

***

Coffee
Petits Fours
Warres 1975 Hine Cognac

Of course, all this is a prelude to the multitude of speeches destined to follow. In recent years, the Lord Mayor's welcome and the Prime Minister's key note speech takes place before dessert, ostensibly so that this State of the Nation address can be broadcast on television at 9pm. But, as has been proven by the nine o'clock news ceasing to exist, the pause in the feasting is really intended to ensure the Lord Mayor and assembled company can do justice to his Pudding.

When it comes to food, every Lord Mayor of London I have had the privilege to cook for has proved to be receptive, appreciative, utterly charming but with very strong views on dessert. The charming Sir John Chalstrey insisted on serving his nursery favourite; Bread and Butter Pudding with Custard, and it took some persuading to be allowed to adulterate the dish with the additions of fresh grape and orange zest. Sir Michael Oliver chose steaming Treacle Puddings complete with dry ice smoke as they were paraded to the tables. Sir Gavyn Arthur's unfortunate allergy to red berries grew to a fearsome hatred such that all berries were ordered to be excommunicated from any kitchen in the City. Sir Robert Finch was a Queen of Puddings fan and most recently David Brewer is a good old-fashioned chocoholic. Sod the speeches, bring on the pudding!

CHOCOLATE, PEAR AND FRANGIPANE TART

There was never any doubt the 2005 Lord Mayor's Banquet would culminate in chocolate but the menu selection tasting was a sight to behold. Steamed chocolate puddings, triple chocolate mousses, chocolate fondants and chocolate trios. This, however, was the eventual winner and when you make it yourself I am sure you will see why.

INGREDIENTS FOR 8
250g flour
85g castor sugar
125g unsalted butter, softened
1 egg
125g marzipan
2 pears

FOR THE FILLING:
300g dark chocolate
230ml double cream
130ml milk
2 eggs
2 tbsp. brandy

METHOD
- Place the flour, sugar, butter and one egg in a food processor or mixer and blend until the pastry is just coming together.
- Turn out on to a floured surface and knead into a ball.
- Line a 25cm loose-bottomed flan tin with baking paper, roll the pastry out into a circle approximately 5cm wider than the flan tin then carefully lift into the tin making sure it is pushed into the edges.
- Prick the base all over then bake blind* in the oven at 200°C for 10 minutes. Remove the 'blindfold' and bake open for a further 10 minutes.
- Roll out the marzipan and fit across the base of the pastry case. Peel and core the pears, cut lengthways into 6 pieces each and arrange on top of the marzipan around the outer edge of the tart.
- In a saucepan, scald the milk and the cream together. Take off the heat. Add the chocolate and stir until melted then mix the eggs with the brandy and add. Pour the mixture over the pears and bake the tart in the oven at 150°C for approximately 40 minutes until just set.
- Serve warm with whipped cream or ice cream.

*For the uninitiated, 'baking blind' is the culinary process you have witnessed when your mother fills the inside of a pastry case with greaseproof paper and rather old uncooked rice.

BREAD AND BUTTER PUDDING

An English classic invented to use up stale buttered bread left over from tea. Here we have added grapes and citrus to freshen and add tang but I hope not spoil the old-school favourite.

INGREDIENTS FOR 6

12 slices of white bread
60g butter, softened
80g sultanas
rind of 1 lemon
rind of 1 orange
150g green seedless grapes

50g demerara sugar
3 eggs
5 tbsp. castor sugar
a pinch of nutmeg
900ml milk

METHOD

- Butter the bread, remove the crusts and cut each slice into four triangles.
- Arrange the bread pieces in a 1 litre ovenproof dish slightly overlapping. Sprinkle with half the sultanas, half the rind from the citrus fruit, half the grapes and half the demerara sugar.
- Cover with another layer of bread and layer again with the remaining fruit mixture
- Finally, top with the remaining triangles of bread.
- Beat the eggs, castor sugar, nutmeg and milk together and pour over the pudding.
- Bake in a preheated oven at 180°C for about 30 minutes.

ANTONY WORRALL THOMPSON'S SPOTTED DICK

An unfortunate title but a really delicious nursery pudding updated with the additions of fresh blueberries and dried cherries. I have yet to hear of a Lord Mayor brave enough to select it for his banquet menu, but this is definitely the sort of dish they favour.

INGREDIENTS FOR 6

100g self raising flour	25g fresh blueberries
a pinch of salt	25g dried cherries
100g fresh white breadcrumbs	25g currants
100g suet	rind of 1 lemon
50g castor sugar	150ml full fat milk

METHOD

- Sift flour and salt into a bowl. Add the breadcrumbs, suet, sugar, blueberries, dried cherries, currants and lemon rind. Mix well.
- Stir in enough milk to make a dropping consistency.
- Spoon mixture into a well buttered 1 litre china pudding basin. Cover with buttered greaseproof paper. Tie securely.
- Steam gently for 2 hours in a saucepan with boiling water one third up the sides of the basin, topping up with more boiling water as required.
- Remove paper and turn out the pudding.
- Serve with thick rich custard or double cream.

TREACLE SPONGE PUDDING

A real 'boys' pudding – classically served with thick yellow custard but I prefer it with the contrast of lemon ice cream.

INGREDIENTS FOR 6

200ml golden syrup – 100ml for baking, 100ml for serving
225g butter, softened
225g sugar
4 eggs

115g self raising flour
115g fresh breadcrumbs
2 lemons, rind and juice
2 tbsp. medium sherry

METHOD FOR SPONGE PUDDING

- Grease a 3 pint pudding basin and spoon 100ml of the golden syrup into the bottom.
- In a food mixer beat the butter and sugar together until light and fluffy then add the eggs and flour a little at a time alternately to combine.
- Stir in the breadcrumbs, lemon rind, juice and the sherry.
- Cover with greaseproof paper and tin foil, tie securely then steam in a bain-marie with water two thirds up the sides for 2½ hours. Keep topping up the water so it doesn't boil dry.
- Heat the remaining golden syrup gently in a pan and allow to cook to a darker, thicker treacle.
- Turn the pudding out on to a serving dish and pour over the treacle.

LEMON ICE CREAM

INGREDIENTS
6 egg yolks
225g sugar
100ml milk
300ml double cream
2 lemons, rind and juice

METHOD
- Beat the egg yolks and sugar together using an electric mixer until they are pale and have doubled in volume.
- Scald the milk in a pan and pour slowly into the egg and sugar mixture beating continually.
- Beat for a further 5 minutes. In a separate bowl whip the cream until it is stiff then fold it into the egg mixture along with the lemon rind and juice.
- Transfer to a container or serving dish and freeze overnight.

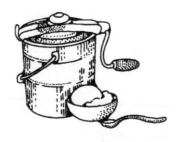

TONY BLAIR'S ALL-IN-ONE CHOCOLATE SPONGE

When the Prime Minister very kindly contributed this as his favourite recipe, I was too polite to enquire whether he actually makes it himself, or Cherie makes it, or even the children make it, or is it simply made for him on the odd occasion when he has time for afternoon tea at No.10?

INGREDIENTS FOR 8

110g self-raising flour (sifted)
1 tsp. baking powder
110g soft margarine
110g castor sugar
2 large eggs

1 tbsp. cocoa powder
125g jam or lemon curd
200ml double cream, whipped
icing sugar

METHOD

- Pre-heat oven to gas mark 3, 170°C.
- Oil and line 2 x 18cm sponge tins with baking paper. • Sift the flour and baking powder into a large mixing bowl.
- Add the other ingredients and whisk with an electric hand whisk until all combined and smooth – the mixture needs to be sloppy so you may need to add a few teaspoons of warm water.
- Divide the mixture into both tins, level off and bake for about 30 minutes.
- Turn out on to cooling racks and remove the lining paper.
- Sandwich together with jam or lemon curd, whipped cream and dust with icing sugar.

CHAPTER 18

A HECKLING OCCASION

> *"...the rich ate and drank freely, accepting gout and apoplexy as things that ran mysteriously in respectable families."*
>
> – *GEORGE ELIOT*

The livery companies of the City of London date back over eight hundred years and are steeped in history (in addition to various other alcoholic cooking liquids). It is fascinating to discover how their heritage has in many ways become part of everyday life and even the English language.

For example, the expression to be 'at sixes and sevens' derives from an ancient feud between The Skinners' Company and The Merchant Taylors. In medieval London, these two distinguished guilds literally resorted to street battles along Cannon Street to dispute who should rightfully be number six in the hierarchy of the Great Twelve Liveries and who should be number seven. Lord Mayor Robert Billesdon in 1484 proposed an inspired solution: the two companies would take it in turns to lead each other in The Lord Mayor's Procession and alternate number each year. As we are discovering, in true City tradition, they still dine together at the Billesdon Dinner each year to celebrate the resolution of their differences.

The Worshipful Company of Clothworkers (number twelve in the livery companies League table) have also had their differences with their rivals, the Dyers, who alas are number thirteen and therefore excluded from the Great Twelve. The Dyers' Company took great exception to this, for several centuries they refused to associate with, or even acknowledge the Clothworkers. Fortunately, this dispute was also resolved and now these two companies dine together once a year to 'bury the hatchet', at their Hatchet Luncheon. One year, the Master Clothworker wishing to drive his point home, commissioned me to make miniature hatchet shaped ginger shortbread biscuits so that each guest received their own hatchet firmly embedded in their Chocolate and Cointreau Truffle Dessert.

To an outsider, a City Livery Dinner would present itself on first site as a very formal austere occasion. Even today, white tie and tails evening dress is often worn, there are strict seating plans in hierarchical order, distinguished guests give learned and witty after dinner speeches and the evening is punctuated by carefully ordered set piece traditions and ceremonies. It is hard to imagine these are the same dinners that prided themselves in drunkenness and debauchery two hundred years ago – or is it?

A truly eminent livery company (where half the members are titled and therefore the identity better remain my secret), has only recently introduced a dining rule that waiters are to ignore requests for additional bread rolls any later than the soup course, and that napkins must be cleared immediately after the 'savoury'. This is so that neither of these things can be used as missiles during the Master's procession! How like a public school dining hall can you get?

Another delightful example of City eccentricity is the Guild of Parish Clerks; an organisation true to its vocation made up entirely of the clerks of London parishes. In medieval times when brethren encountered a fellow clerk on the streets of London, they would greet one another by calling out their parish titles rather that their real names. For example: "Hail St James Dukes Place" would receive a reply of "Greetings St Botolph without Aldgate", The Parish Clerks now regularly dine together in the City and in the middle of the meal (whilst my soufflé may be collapsing or my sorbet may be melting) they pause for a toast. The first toast is quite normal and is addressed to a new member (by name of the parish, of course). Then randomly, two or three other clerks rise to propose their own toasts, shouting over one another to be heard. In the end every single member is rising to his feet and repeatedly bellowing their toasts to others across the dining room. It sounds as though a mutiny has set in, and that we, as caterers, should quickly clear the tables of breakable objects, disperse the crowd and send everyone home. The riotous noise continues for several minutes before hoarse and exhausted, diners slowly resume their seats and the ruckus dies away.

At last normality returns and a reviving boozy dessert must be served. Here are some lovely alcoholic pudding recipes; you will need to practice hard, however, to recreate the heckling to go with them.

PORT AND PLUM TRIFLE

It is virtually sacrilege in the City of London not to drink port but I am one of the unbelievers and think that the only good use for the stray bottle in the cupboard is a traditional boozy trifle. You will also need that fabulous old crystal bowl Great Aunt left you to ensure you achieve real Mrs Beeton style.

INGREDIENTS FOR 6-8
10 plums – 8 for trifle and 2
   for decoration
1 sheet of sponge base or 10
   trifle sponge fingers
60g castor sugar
1 small jar plum jam
80ml port
300ml double cream –
   whipped
mint sprigs & angelica to
   decorate

FOR THE CUSTARD
450ml milk
3 egg yolks
1 heaped tbsp. cornflour
3 tbsp. castor sugar
vanilla essence
zest of 1 orange

METHOD FOR CUSTARD
- Heat milk in a pan and bring up to scalding point.
- In a bowl, mix egg yolks, cornflour, castor sugar, vanilla essence and orange zest.
- Add the egg mix to the milk and stir over a gentle heat until it thickens.

METHOD FOR TRIFLE
- Quarter 8 of the plums and stew them in a small saucepan with the castor sugar until soft.
- Spread plum jam on to sponge cake and cut into fingers.
- In a glass bowl, build up layers of plums and sponge fingers.
- Spoon over the port and then the custard, ensuring it dribbles down the edges and into all the gaps.
- Chill in the fridge for 2–3 hours.
- To finish, pipe whipped cream on top and decorate with fresh plum slices, angelica and mint leaves.

HERBERT BERGER'S WARM STRAWBERRIES IN SAUTERNES WITH BLACK PEPPER

I mischievously wonder why Herbert Berger recipes always involve very good quality wines and what he suggests we should do with the rest of the bottle. This, however, is a delightful little dish and I am sure you can think of something to do with the remaining Sauternes. I would serve the warm strawberries with some oozy ripe Camembert rather than ice cream but try for yourself.

INGREDIENTS FOR 6
900g strawberries
½ bottle good sweet wine
a pinch of cracked black pepper

METHOD
- Warm the sauternes in a pan with the black pepper and infuse for about 5 minutes.
- Add the strawberries and bring to the boil but do not overcook, they should be firm and still cold in the middle.
- Serve immediately with either vanilla ice cream or fresh cream.

CHOCOLATE FONDANT WITH MADEIRA SYLLABUB

This is that yummy chocolate pudding which when you cut into it has a rich, runny centre. Your guests will think you are very skilled to achieve such a gourmet restaurant dish but the truth is it is just a very rich chocolate cake served half raw.

INGREDIENTS FOR 6
170g butter
170g chocolate drops
130g castor sugar
90g plain flour
20g cocoa
1 tsp. baking powder
3 whole eggs
2 egg yolks

FOR THE SYLLABUB
300ml double cream
2 tbsp. runny honey
50ml Madeira
a pinch of cinnamon juice and zest of 1 lemon

METHOD FOR FONDANT
- Melt butter, chocolate and sugar in a saucepan over a low heat, stirring all the time until completely melted and runny. Transfer to a mixing bowl.
- Sieve together the flour, cocoa and baking powder and fold into the chocolate mixture.
- Stir in the eggs and extra egg yolks – the mixture should be shiny and smooth.
- Butter and dust with cocoa 6 dairole moulds then spoon in the mixture.
- Bake in a preheated oven at 200° for 7 minutes (precisely!).

TO FINISH
- Make the syllabub by simply whisking the double cream until it is stiff then folding in the honey, Madeira, cinnamon and lemon.
- Remove the fondants from the oven. When they are cool enough to handle, turn them out on to individual plates.
- Serve immediately with the syllabub dolloped alongside.

HOT GRAND MARNIER SOUFFLÉ

A hot soufflé is always considered to be the ultimate culinary achievement. It combines a degree of skill, timing and bravery to definitely create the wow factor every chef seeks. The old Master Chef of the Mansion House, Michel Giguel was a great exponent of the souffle?, for many years preparing fish ones, vegetable ones and desserts for each serving Lord Mayor.

INGREDIENTS FOR 6

A little melted butter
3 whole eggs, separated
40g vanilla sugar 2
5g flour, sieved
200ml milk

50ml double cream
zest of 1 orange
zest of 1 lemon
4 tbsp. Grand Marnier
50g castor sugar

METHOD

- Paint six ramekins with melted butter and dust with castor sugar.
- Combine egg yolks and vanilla sugar together until smooth, then add the sieved flour. Beat until smooth.
- Heat the milk and cream to scalding point then pour over the egg mixture. Whisk to remove all the lumps, return the mixture to the saucepan and cook over a gentle heat until thickened and smooth – stirring all the time.
- Transfer to a bowl to cool.
- Stir in the orange and lemon zest and the Grand Marnier.
- In a separate bowl, whisk egg whites until very stiff but not dry and add the castor sugar.
- Fold the meringue mixture into the custard base and spoon into the buttered ramekins. Flatten off the tops with a palette knife.
- Bake at 190°C for 12–15 minutes until risen and golden.
- Serve immediately.

RHUBARB AND ORANGE FOOL WITH
CRYSTALLISED ROSE PETALS

For me, Rhubarb Fool means Spring is here and Summer is on the way. This charming old-fashioned dessert is popular with all ages and decorated with rose petals will be a picture of English elegance.

INGREDIENTS FOR 6
FOR THE CUSTARD
600ml milk
4 egg yolks
2 heaped tbsp. cornflour
3 tbsp. castor sugar
450g rhubarb
2 oranges, grated rind and
    juice
60g castor sugar
300ml double cream

FOR THE ROSE PETALS
2 pink roses
1 egg white
castor sugar to dredge

METHOD FOR CUSTARD
- Heat the milk in a pan and bring up to scalding point.
- In a bowl, mix the egg yolks, cornflour and castor sugar. Add the egg mix to the milk and stir over a gentle heat until it thickens. Transfer to a large bowl and allow it to cool.

METHOD FOR RHUBARB AND ORANGE
- Cut the rhubarb into 5cm long sticks and place in a saucepan with the orange juice and castor sugar. Cook gently until the rhubarb is soft then leave to cool.
- Lightly whip the cream and fold it into the cold custard along with the rhubarb and orange rind. Do not over fold, it can still be quite mottled.
- Spoon into a serving dish and garnish with rose petals.

METHOD FOR ROSE PETALS
- These need to be made 24 hours in advance!
- Separate out the petals and brush with lightly whisked egg whites. Dredge with castor sugar and leave to dry overnight in a cool place.

CHAPTER 19

PASS THE PORT: A TOASTING TRADITION

"Well, many's the long night I've dreamed of cheese – toasted mostly." – ROBERT LOUIS STEVENSON

'Pray Silence for the Loyal Toast' – When is toast not something delicious spread with butter and Marmite? The origins of 'toasting' by drinking to an assembled company is fascinating and really does relate back to a piece of crispy grilled bread.

In the 16th Century it became customary to put a piece of toasted bread into wine or beer as a sort of built-in snack like adding crouton to soup. 'Drinking a Toast' then became the fashion and any excuse would do to down alcoholic drinks (and presumably soggy rusks) as a salute to persons present, persons absent or events. Toastmasters came into existence as a sort of game referee on duty to ensure everyone got their turn at proposing their own toast. Gentlemen of the City would drink to a woman's beauty from their slipper or cut their arm and add blood to their beverage to toast a young lady offering proof of their love.

Thankfully, some of these customs have disappeared, but toasting remains an integral part of City dining. The City of London's most unique toast is to:

> "Drink to you in a loving cup
> and bid you all a hearty welcome."

There follows a cumbersome, traditional ceremony during which large gold or silver chalices filled with spiced wine (The Loving Cups) are passed to each guest in turn to drink from. Three people stand, two face each other, bow, then whilst one removes the lid of the cup, holding it high in the air, the central person drinks then wipes the cup with an attached napkin. The third, meanwhile, has his back to the drinker in order to protect him from unexpected attack whilst he imbibes. (Clear so far?) The protector then sits, the first drinker turns to protect, the lid man turns and takes his turn at the cup and the next person at the table stands to lift the lid. And so on around the tables until everyone has partaken. If you are confused by this clear explanation on paper, imagine the chaos which ensues when new members of some inspired modern guild such as The Worshipful Company of Environmental Cleaners or the Guild of Security Professionals get together and after several hours of drinking attempt the ceremony.

A much more obscure but equally fascinating drinking ritual is unique to the Clothworkers' Company where as a guest at dinner a wine waiter will ask: "Do you dine with Alderman or Lady Cooper?" Record has it that on St Thomas Eve in 1664 Alderman Sir William Cooper collapsed at the Clothworkers' dinner. His hosts attempted to revive him with brandy but he died. The following day, Lady Cooper came to reprimand the Clothworkers saying that had they offered her husband his customary remedy, Holland gin, he would have recovered. She then gave the company a bursary to ensure that gin would be offered as an alternative to brandy in perpetuity. And to this day, every guest at every major Clothworkers' dinner is asked the obscure question to choose between brandy or gin.

'Regimental Fire' is the toast given by members to fellow members of the Honourable Artillery Company – the City's ancient army regiment based at Armoury House in City Road. It takes the form of a nine fold shout of the word "Zay" together with some obscure arm movements. Apparently it originates from when all good chaps would be given three cheers (or in this case 'Zays') and particularly good chaps (e.g. members of the HAC) would be given three times three cheers, hence nine. As a guest, not a member, you will be toasted with 'Silent Fire' – still lots of arm movements but only a single 'Zay' on the ninth thrust.

Perhaps the most familiar British drinking tradition is to pass the port. Whilst other drinks may be poured by servants, butlers, footmen, stewards, waiters or sommeliers; port must always be passed. I was only eighteen when, as the youngest person present, I found myself in a very formal dining room seated next to my hostess at a great polished dining table adorned with huge silver candelabra and table centrepieces. At the end of the meal the ladies withdrew to do whatever it is they do and have liqueurs in the (with)drawing room. A crystal decanter of vintage port was then placed directly in front of me. I have never been good with rights and lefts and although I knew enough to know I was expected to help myself then pass it on I was unsure of direction. Luckily with a 50/50 chance, I passed the decanter to the nice old gentlemen on my left. He nodded approvingly, helped himself and having clearly detected my hesitation proceeded to tell us that on board ships once at sea, the port is passed the other way. Now I was really confused.

The gastronomic argument of whether port should only be served after a meal is finished or is the perfect accompaniment to "savouries" is one I cannot adjudicate. The City has a great tradition of serving a cheesy, spicy or meaty delicacy at the end of a banquet and if you wish to drink rich sweet fortified wine with it then why not. Here are some classic savoury course recipes to help you along.

The Lord Mayor's Coach

SCOTCH WOODCOCK

A very traditional City favourite – this is really a type of rich creamy scrambled eggs with anchovy. There must be something about eating very salty fish in order to encourage port drinking. For me, a crisp Vino Verde or Pinot Grigio to cut the spicy cream filled dish would be much more appropriate, but it is not to be.

INGREDIENTS FOR 6
6 egg yolks
salt and pepper
pinch of cayenne
500ml double cream
6 slices of bread
25g butter
18 anchovy fillets
chopped parsley and paprika to garnish

METHOD
- Whisk together the egg yolks, salt, pepper, cayenne and double cream in a large bowl.
- Set the bowl over a pan of boiling water and cook slowly stirring regularly until the mixture begins to thicken but not set.
- Toast and butter the bread, trimming off the crusts and cut into triangles.
- Spoon the egg mixture on to the toast. Garnish with anchovy fillets, chopped parsley and paprika.

WELSH RAREBIT

A tasty savoury at the end of a banquet or a satisfying Sunday night supper in front of the fire; Welsh Rarebit is a traditional dish that requires no modernising or updating. With the addition of a fried egg on top you have a 'Buck Rarebit', though why the buck produces the egg I cannot tell you.

INGREDIENTS FOR 6

3 tbsp. butter
3 tbsp. flour
440ml milk
200ml beer
1 tsp. English mustard
½ tsp. Worcestershire sauce

¼ tsp. cayenne pepper
340g cheddar cheese, grated
3 egg yolks
6 slices of bread toasted or 3
  split toasted muffins

METHOD

- Melt the butter in a medium saucepan. Stir in the flour and cook over a medium heat for 2 minutes, stirring constantly.
- Slowly pour in the milk and bring to the boil stirring all the time.
- Next, add the beer, mustard, Worcestershire sauce and cayenne pepper, reduce the heat and simmer for a couple of minutes.
- Add the cheese a handful at a time stirring until melted then remove from the heat and beat in the egg yolks. Check seasoning.
- Spread the mixture on to toast and finish under the grill until golden brown.

MATURE CHEDDAR SOUFFLÉ

As you may have guessed from their frequent appearance in this book I am something of a soufflé fan. They can be fishy, vegetable baked, sweet or savoury. There is nothing, however, that can beat a classic cheese soufflé just risen and served with an extra bottle of Red Burgundy.

INGREDIENTS FOR 6

30g butter
30g plain flour
150ml milk
salt and pepper

½ tsp. cayenne pepper
½ tsp. dijon mustard
180g mature cheddar, grated
6 eggs, separated

METHOD

- Melt the butter in a saucepan, add the flour and allow to cook for a couple of minutes. Then add the milk and stir until thickened.
- Season with salt, pepper, cayenne and mustard. Add the cheese and stir until it has melted.
- Remove from the heat and blend in the egg yolks.
- Whisk the egg whites into stiff peaks and fold into the cheese mixture. Ladle into a 1 litre soufflé dish.
- Bake in the oven at 200°C for 30–35 minutes.

BAKED MUSHROOM WITH STILTON AND REDCURRANT

This is our most popular end of dinner savoury. Even when guests are saying they could not possibly eat another thing, the mixture of the buttery mushrooms, sweet but seasoned redcurrant and strong salty stilton is irresistible.

INGREDIENTS FOR 6
50g butter, melted
6 black field mushrooms 10 cm diameter
salt and pepper
6 tsp. redcurrant jelly
170g blue stilton
chopped parsley

METHOD
- Place the mushrooms on a baking tin and brush with butter. Season with salt and pepper.
- Bake in the oven at 200°C for 10 minutes. Cool a little then drain off the juice.
- Mix the redcurrant jelly with salt and pepper and spoon into the centre of each mushroom.
- Divide the stilton into six and crumble on to each mushroom.
- Bake in the oven for 8–10 minutes until the cheese is bubbly.
- This is perfect served with a lightly dressed leaf salad.

DEVILS ON HORSEBACK

Bacon wrapped morsels have long been popular as savouries, canapés or even starters. They are hugely adaptable and can include kidneys, chicken liver, scallops, apricots or dates. I have been trying to research more heaven, hell or horse related names but without success. We invented a dish called Spiced Bananas in Pyjamas (Bananas wrapped in bacon) perhaps that has some place in purgatory.

INGREDIENTS
24 blanched almonds
24 pitted prunes
12 rashers streaky bacon

METHOD
- Push the blanched almonds into the cavity of the prunes.
- Stretch out the rashers of bacon and cut into two. Lay a prune at one end of each slice and roll up.
- Place on a wire rack with a baking sheet underneath and cook in the oven for 10 minutes.

ANGELS ON HORSEBACK

INGREDIENTS
24 oysters, 'native' no. 3s
12 rashers streaky bacon
salt and pepper

METHOD
- Open the oysters carefully (try not to stab yourself) and remove the flesh from the shell. See chapter 6 for more instructions.
- Stretch out the rashers of bacon and cut into two.
- Lay an oyster on each one and roll up.
- Place on a wire rack with a baking sheet underneath and cook in the oven for 10 minutes.

CHAPTER 20

A RECIPE FOR DISASTERS

I am sure that people kind enough to buy this book in aid of the Treloar Trust will have looked at it in two very different ways. There are those who will not have been bothered with a word of my carefully related stories and anecdotes of the City but instead ransacked the recipes to discover the secrets of culinary success. Was Tony Blair's route to being Prime Minister through his chocolate cake? Will mastering Rick Stein's Crab Florentine enable you to dominate the cooking of an entire country? And having been constantly told how easy all the recipes are, why is there no instruction on how to sue Peter Gladwin for misrepresentation?

Then there is the second category who have studied every word of the text, checking the bits of history against reference books and analysing my psychological profiling of bankers at lunch. Is vintage champagne the perfect partner for Treacle Sponge Pudding? Should you serve spaghetti when you next entertain the Italian President to lunch? And who stole the Queen Mum's wine on her 100th birthday? What both types of reader always want to know, however, is what goes wrong? I have never done a radio interview or daytime TV documentary without being pestered for a good disaster story.

The greatest City dining catastrophe was in 1827 when at the Lord Mayor's Banquet a tremendous raft of oil lamps made in the shape of a huge anchor came crashing down on the top table severely injuring the Lord Mayor, Mathias Prime Lucas, and some of his principal guests. To quote the somewhat understated Annual Register, "the conviviality of the evening was disrupted."

Lord Kingsdown, a former Governor of the Bank of England, has very bravely allowed me to recount his little culinary disaster, an occasion when he was entertaining Princess Margaret in his private dining room at the Bank. As I am sure you are aware, the correct way to offer food to royalty (or for that matter any member of the aristocracy) is called butler service – whereby a 'butler' proffers a dish or platter of food to the guests allowing them to help themselves to as much or as little as they want. I have not been told whether the visit was for a deposit or a withdrawal, but the Governor's Lunch with Her Royal Highness had all gone well up until dessert. Presented with a lovely bowl of ice-cream, the Princess made several attempts to dent it with a spoon but it was frozen in a solid mass. She and the butler eventually agreed it was best she gave up and then all the other guests quickly decided they did not want ice-cream either. This brings me on to our own ice-cream confession about a dinner prepared for the Duke of Edinburgh at St James' Palace. His Peach and Cointreau Ice-Cream Bombe was already on his plate, but not for long. Inserting his royal spoon it leapt off across the table to the guest opposite. Luckily the Prince guffawed and was keen to retrieve it but we replaced it instead.

The Livery Halls of the City are elegant, palatial and self-assured – not the sort of places for disasters. Little do those fortunate to dine in them suspect what goes on behind the green base door whilst they are enjoying gentile conversation and fine food and wine.

View of Blackfriars Bridge and St Paul's Cathedral

The first livery to entertain the Lord Mayor after his appointment to office is always the Carpenters' Company. Proud of this tradition they lay on a lavish multi-course dinner, including on this particular occasion Fillet of Sole with Minted Pea Puree, a recipe already described in this book. Individual plating of a fish course like this for 220 guests is no mean task and must be carried out by a frenetic team of chefs at great speed. The very first cauldron of pea puree, however, was dropped in the middle of the kitchen floor and with no time to tackle the mess, the assembly line operation just repeatedly trod up and down straight through it. The next course, a Baron of Beef was to be paraded on a stretcher and presented to the top table. As my colleague and I processed around the room bearing the beast there was a horrible crack as one arm of the stretcher gave way. The presentation was completed rather awkwardly with a third person supporting at the side and it was only as we did our three legged race march out that I noticed our shoes leaving a trail of pea green slime! The Carpenters did not say a word or perhaps had been unaware of our minor disasters until today.

There have been many similar well hidden disasters. In the days long ago when my wife would come to help out, she bounced a huge whole roast turkey down the back stairs of The Glaziers' Hall. There was little choice but to wash it, bandage it with excessive garnish and serve it – no one was any the wiser. The Plaisterers who possess both the largest and most high-tech Livery Hall in the City had a mains water pipe burst creating a torrential river through their new state of the art kitchen throughout their inaugural banquet. Once again the show must go on and what the customer does not see he does not know.

Some of you may have read in my previous books that my most important piece of advice if things do not go quite right in the kitchen, is to bluff. Always tell your guests how pleased you are with a most unusual culinary creation. This technique, of course, works less well in a professional situation although my own reflex action is still to use the same defence. In the face of an abusive head waiter who is the bearer of complaints from the dining room, I would gulp down mugs full of wildly over-peppered soup to prove its palatability, or relentlessly chew the toughest piece of steak to prove its tenderness. At home you must do the same. Who is to say you did not invent Dauphinois Potato Brûlée? Why not be the orig-inator of sweet scrambled egg instead of confessing you have curdled the custard? Set a new trend in Carpaccio of raw duck and blame the dentures not the dish. Stand up, be proud of your cooking, be brazen in the face of disaster.

The following are not recipes for disasters but oddities which certainly have their place in the City but have not quite fitted in to any other chapter. I hope you enjoy these and all the other tales of cooking, miscellaneous facts and recipes contained in this book. Thank you again for supporting The Treloar Trust.

"The biggest seller is cookbooks and the second is diet books – how not to eat what you've just learned how to cook." – *ANDY ROONEY*

QUINCE AND THYME JELLY

There is something very English about serving jam with meat and in this cosmopolitan city of jus, salsas and reductions it is a tradition we should hang on to. This particular jelly is also excellent with hot cheese savoury dishes.

INGREDIENTS
4 jars
1.75kg quinces
3 lemons, rind and juice
3½ litres water
1.25kg preserving sugar
8 sprigs of fresh thyme

METHOD
- Wash and chop the quince, all pips and core should be left in.
- Place the quinces in a large saucepan, cover with 2½ litres of water and simmer for 1 hour until tender. Strain through a jelly bag and reserve the liquid. Return the pulp to the pan, add the remaining water and bring to the boil. Simmer for a further 30 minutes and strain again. This time discard the fruit pulp.
- Measure the total volume of liquid and weigh out the sugar : 450g of sugar to 500ml of liquid.
- Place in a pan and boil vigorously to reduce by half until setting point is reached, removing any scum as it rises to the top. To test, the jelly should appear firm when poured on to a cold plate.
- Sterilise jam jars and place 2 sprigs of thyme in each. Pour in the jelly mix – cover and seal the top.

POTTED CHEESE AND MELBA TOAST

A favourite first course, last course or snack served with pickled onions, celery and pints of best bitter. Keeps for several weeks in the fridge as long as the butter seal is not broken.

INGREDIENTS FOR 6

450g cheddar, grated	3 tbsp. melted butter
175g butter, softened	9 slices of white bread
1 tsp. mustard powder	¼ tsp. cayenne pepper
½ tsp. powdered mace	150ml sweet sherry or brandy
½ tsp. Worcestershire sauce	

METHOD

- Combine the cheese, butter, mustard powder and mace in a food processor. Season with cayenne pepper and Worcestershire sauce then gradually add the sherry or brandy until it is creamy and smooth.
- Press the mixture into 6 ramekins or 1 larger pot, pour over the melted butter and allow to set.

METHOD FOR MELBA TOAST

- Preheat the grill and toast the bread lightly on both sides. Cut off the crusts and then holding the toast flat, split the bread in half.
- Cut each piece into 2 triangles and toast the uncooked sides until they are golden brown and the edges start to curl.

WATERMELON AND LEMONADE CRUSH

The colour alone is nearly enough to tempt me away from booze – although not quite. This is, however, a lovely Summer soft drink perfect for children, drivers or those who simply don't.

INGREDIENTS
6 glasses
2 lemons
½ small watermelon
115g castor sugar
crushed ice
lemon balm to decorate

METHOD
- Chop the lemons into small pieces. Take the skin off the watermelon and cut into chunks. Place both fruits in a food processor with the sugar and a small amount of water. Process until the lemons are pulped.
- Pass the mixture through a sieve, squeezing out as much juice as possible .Top up with cold water to make up to 1200ml. Refrigerate until needed.
- Serve with plenty of ice and sprigs of lemon balm or mint.

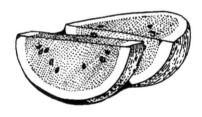

APRICOT AND ORANGE CHUTNEY

There is something both satisfying and therapeutic about making your own chutneys. It is one of those back to our roots, feathering the nest type of activities, and why not – a perfect activity for a rainy afternoon.

INGREDIENTS

800g apricots, stoned & quartered
300g cooking apples, peeled & cubed
2 oranges, zest and juice
500g soft brown sugar
800ml cider vinegar

2 onions, finely chopped
2 cloves garlic, finely chopped
200g sultanas
1 tbsp. ground ginger
2 tsp. salt
2 cinnamon sticks

METHOD

- Place the apricots, apple, orange, sugar and vinegar in a saucepan and stir over a low heat until the sugar has dissolved.
- Add all the other ingredients and bring to the boil, lower the heat and simmer gently for 1½–2 hours, stirring occasionally.
- The chutney should be a thick, soft consistency and will thicken more as it cools.
- Pour into warm jars, top with wax disks and seal with screw top lids.

* Fruit chutneys like this can be made with all sorts of different ingredients including plums, pears, grapes and gooseberries.

NOT SIR JOHN MAJOR'S FIZZ – ELDERFLOWER CHAMPAGNE INSTEAD

Sir John Major spent weeks corresponding with us on what his story, anecdote or recipe contribution would be and then at last presented 'a slush puppy for the very rich.' Extremely expensive Laurent Perrier Rosé Champagne frozen then eaten. Personally I can think of better things to do with that particular lovely drink so I am sorry Sir John, here is my mother's Elderflower Champagne instead.

INGREDIENTS
10 heads of elderflowers, picked from the hedgerows in May or
  early June
1 lemon, juice only
450g granulated sugar
2 tbsp. white wine vinegar
4½ litres water

METHOD
- Place all the ingredients into a large saucepan, stir and bring up to the boil.
- Remove from the heat and leave to steep for 24 hours.
- Strain out the flowers and decant the liquid into bottles with traditional flip-top stoppers (you may need to drink a few Grolsch lagers!)
- Leave for 2–3 weeks for the 'champagne' to become fizzy.

"Prosperity to the City of London and its cooking, may it flourish, root and branch forever." – New City Toast.

INDEX